Three Wives for the Planter

Three Wives for the Planter

PAMELA ROPER-CALDBECK

with original illustrations by
CYRIL SHUTLER

Pam R.C.

SERENDIPITY

First published in 2002 by
Serendipity
Suite 530
37 Store Street
Bloomsbury
London

British Library Cataloguing-in-Publication data
A catalogue record for this book is available from the British Library

ISBN 1-84394-000-0

Printed and bound by Alden Digital, Oxford

For my Roper-Caldbeck grandchildren,
Nicholas, Shaun, Rebecca, James, Holly,
Barnaby, Tessa, Olivia,
and great-grandchildren
Tristan, Olivia, Jasper

Part One
Malaya in the 1920s

WE HAD ARRIVED AT LAST. The train journey from Singapore had taken four hours. It was only one hundred miles, but we had stopped at least eight times at the small stations along the line. These had fascinated us. The mail train from Singapore to Kuala Lumpur was a daily event, and so the local populace came down to meet it, partly to gossip to any friends they might find on board, and in particular to see who was in the first class carriages.

White women were very rare, so this had obviously been a very special day for them. To find three at one go was too good to be true, and they crowded round the windows which were wide open. We smiled and waved to show we were at least human, but this only produced embarrassed giggles. The language was a mixture of Malay, Tamil and Chinese, so it all sounded double Dutch to us.

Labis was *our* destination, and here everything was in an uproar. All the Tamil labour from the estate – well over a hundred – plus a swarm of children had come to meet their Master returning from a holiday in his own country with, so rumour had it, not only one wife, but three. Presumably my mother was the head one, with my sister Joan number two, and myself, aged ten, very much last. Already extremely hot and moist, we got out of the train to be nearly felled by the oven-like temperature. We donned our topees as drilled by Charles and waited while Mr Sammagara, the chief clerk, made a welcoming speech in English, and garlanded us all with gardenias, already going brown at their edges and overpoweringly scented. The crowd yelled their enthusiasm, and as many of them had been born on the estate, some had never seen a white woman and certainly not at such close quarters. All the same it was obvious that they approved of the way their Master had ended his bachelorhood in no uncertain manner. After all, to them he was a very rich man and what better way of spending his money?

Mrs Sammagara had made new covers for the cushions in the dogcart, brilliant blue with orange frills. The horse, affected by the general excitement, was raring to go, while our mother and Charles were trying to make the front seats, Joan and I scrambled up behind, giggling weakly and slightly hysterical. We nearly fell out as we bounded forward with all the children running after us, and Charles shouted over his shoulder to tell the little devils to go to hell. We gathered that in Tamil this was: '*po nee mudian*' (go you fools) which made us laugh all the more. At last we were clear of them, and went spanking down the village street, followed by the stares of the Chinese shopkeepers. Soon we passed an entrance with a large notice board saying 'North Labis Rubber Estate', and about a quarter of a mile further we turned up a steep drive, through a white painted gate, to a big two-storied bungalow, surrounded by a very lush and beautiful garden.

The house servants were waiting to greet us. They had all been with my step-father for years, and consisted of three Chinese: a cook, number one boy and number two boy. All of them were well over thirty, and the cook nearer fifty, but they were all known as *boys.* They were a nice friendly lot and put on a brave face at the invasion, although probably more than apprehensive at the thought of their peaceful life of looking after one man being shattered by us females. However, they launched themselves into a flood of excited Malay, and this was added to by two madly barking dogs. They were smooth-haired fox-terriers, mother and son, called Lady and Pups. Charles had warned us to be careful of the old lady, as he called her, as he thought she might resent us and be jealous, but he need not have worried as she took to my mother at once, and seldom left her side after the first few days. I had always wanted a dog of my own, so was thrilled when Pups attached himself to me.

As well as the Chinese boys, there was a Tamil water-carrier, called the 'Tunkan Ayer', as there was no plumbing except for a cold water tap in the bathroom. His job was to carry up hot water for the baths, and to remove the lavatory bins known as *jampans.* He spent the rest of his time doing odd jobs or helping the gardener, another Tamil, and rather a sad, pathetic looking little man, but they were both so eager to please that we became very fond of them. We soon made ourselves understood by *dum carmbo*, and the few words we picked up.

The bungalow was very cool and airy as all the rooms upstairs were surrounded by open verandahs, and the bedrooms had swing doors, open at the top and bottom, so you could see people's legs and the top of their heads, but they gave one a certain amount of privacy. A large sitting-room in the centre stretched right across the house, and this we used all the time, although there was another smaller one downstairs on the opposite side to the dining-room. There was also a guest bedroom and bath there.

Our bedrooms were either side of the main sitting-room, both with their own bathrooms tiled to the ceiling. The rooms seemed huge to us, but big rooms with high ceilings were cooler, and in the extreme heat this was very important. All the rooms had fans suspended in the centre which were worked by the electricity plant in the factory some miles away. The only snag was that on most nights it ceased to work after 10.00 p.m. unless there was a dinner party when Charles would have it kept on until whatever hour he wanted the guests to leave.

The garden was over an acre, with lawns of very coarse grass and lots of flowering trees and shrubs, including the lovely pale blue plumbago, hibiscus in every shade of pink, and both pink and white frangipani with their single wax-like flowers. In the middle of the main lawn was a jacaranda tree which dropped its mauvy blue blossom in a circle round the trunk reminding us of bluebells. Coconut trees grew along the fringe of the tennis court, but the whole garden was surrounded by rubber trees. Everything remained very green all the year round because of the damp heat and plentiful rainfall. There were masses of birds, some very brightly coloured, and parrakeets gathered at dusk in the coconut trees and would fly across the lawn in hundreds.

Our lives soon got into a daily pattern. There was no outlet from the place except by rail, so the few Europeans on the two estates were thrown on each other for company. The three young men who worked as assistants to Charles were all bachelors. The oldest and most serious minded of the three was John Gearing; he was good looking and although not much over thirty was already going grey. Fred Ward came from Yorkshire and was small and fair with a cheerful red face; a complete opposite to Ralph Batts who was tall and very thin, with dark patent-leather hair. He laughed a lot and seemed to enjoy life and was always ready for a party. Soon they were all treating Mummy as their 'father-confessor', and her arrival on the scene must have made a lot of difference to their lives. She was a sympathetic listener, and they were all a long way from home and lonely.

Joan, who was nineteen and considered very pretty, would obviously have been the centre of their interests if it had not been that on the boat out from England she had lost her heart to John Cutler, who was on his way out to join a firm of rubber brokers in Singapore. He was certainly every maiden's dream of the tall, dark and handsome stranger. For some unknown reason they failed to exchange addresses when we left the ship thinking, I suppose, in their lovelorn state, that the life on board would last for ever. There is nothing quite so shattering as the abrupt ending of a sea voyage, and when we got to Raffles Hotel, where

On the boat to Singapore (1923), Joan, John and the author.

we were to spend our first two nights, Joan was suddenly overcome by the thought that she had lost John for ever. She lay on the bed, dressed in a pink satin evening dress, sobbing her heart out. My mother frantically tried to console her, by saying he was certain to turn up the next day, and could she not pull herself together sufficiently to go downstairs to have dinner with some of Charles's friends who had come to meet him and were agog to see his beautiful step-daughter.

At last, red-eyed and completely silent, she agreed to go and I was left in the huge hotel bedroom alone. I was quite happy about this as I felt bewildered by all the drama, and secretly thought Joan was making a lot of fuss about nothing. I was just ten and longing to explore, especially the exciting looking bathroom which was reached down a long flight of steps from the bedroom. This was no ordinary affair as one washed in a small tin tub, which the boy, when requested, filled with hot water. This was meant to be done standing up, although I was still small enough to squeeze myself down, in a sitting position. After this one dipped a container into an 'Ali Baba' type of jar filled with cold water, and poured it over oneself. Even in that heat this took a bit of nerve, but after the first one it was heaven, and such fun to be able to throw water all over the floor. This was made of cement and at a slight slope, so the water disappeared down a drain.

I could see over the verandah down to the lawn below where people were dining out in the open. The tables were wired to electric candles, the shades casting pools of pink light. The party was apparently in full swing, although Joan did not seem to be contributing much to the fun. However, the next morning all was well, as John had tracked us down to 'John Little's', the big store where everyone went to drink coffee. They could only be secretly engaged, as his firm did not allow their young assistants to marry until they had served two years. So it was arranged that John would come up to Labis whenever he could, which meant most weekends and all the numerous public holidays.

We loved the life on the estate. It was so completely different to anything we had known, and we were intrigued with everything. One of our amusements was naming the various Indian men who came up to the house, after people we had known at home. A lot of Tamil men had long hair done up in little buns on the top of their heads and this, with their sarongs and delicate European features, gave them a very effeminate appearance. One in particular who brought the post reminded us of our cook Mabel. This we called him to his face and he answered to it quite happily. The small boys, known as *Podiuns*, who came up to ball-boy when we played tennis, were also nicknamed after various friends in England, mostly girls, but of course they did not realise this. They also often had long hair, and all were very dark skinned.

The day started at 6.00 a.m. when Charles had his morning cup of tea and fruit out on the verandah. I would join him. It was a fascinating time to be up, as it was cool and fresh, sometimes a little misty, but always warm enough for very little clothing. The monkeys, who lived in the jungle just the other side of the railway line, would be calling to each other in their lovely high-pitched liquid notes until the sun began to get really hot, around 8.00 a.m. Charles would be out at 6.30 a.m. taking the dogs with him and generally walking, although he would take the dog cart if he wanted to inspect any work going on some way from the bungalow, or pay a visit to the factory.

I often went with him as I liked to watch the men tapping the trees. They cut the old layer of rubber left behind from the day before, which would then start the liquid rubber running into the little china cups attached to the trees by wire frames. Later the women would go round with two buckets hung on a yoke across their shoulders, and collect the 'milk' and take it to the factory where it was put in large tanks to congeal. This was the end of their work for the day and by 12.30 p.m., they would return home and spend the afternoon sleeping until it was cooler, when the men would go and play football or tend their gardens while the women got the evening meal.

Twice a week the 'Toddy' shop, or local pub, would be open and this was attended by both sexes. The 'lines' where they all lived were long houses, four or five families to each, divided up into two rooms, sleeping quarters and kitchen, with a communicating verandah. These were no distance from the bungalow, and we could hear the various rows that went on, and the endless beat of the tom-toms that were played at any excuse. There was a *mandore* or foreman who was meant to keep order, but if he failed to settle any disputes – and these after a toddy or two often resulted in drawn knives – he would call Charles who, in fluent Tamil, would go down and put the fear of God into them, so he said, but this was only the last resort from the *mandore*'s point of view as it meant he lost 'face'.

During the time between breakfast – for which Charles returned about 9.00 a.m. – and lunch, I was 'educated' by Joan and Mummy. They used a mixture of P.N.E.U. and their own ingenuity, which in after years took some sorting out but on the whole stood me in good stead, in particular the Friday's general knowledge paper for which even Charles was called upon to make suggestions. In the afternoon we were meant to 'lie off', on our beds or, in Mummy's and Charles's case, on long wicker chairs placed on the verandah outside their bedroom. Sometimes Charles returned to the office at the bottom of the drive where the two clerks stayed until 4.00 p.m. each day. This was the accepted thing for non-manual workers.

I would spend a lot of this time writing, and later produced a newspaper called the *Labis News*, all in longhand and only one copy which went the rounds among the assistants. I also wrote long letters to the friends I had left behind in England, and to several pen-friends acquired through the pages of a children's magazine and who were scattered all over the world. We read a good deal and the books were sent down by rail in a wooden container from the library at Kuala Lumpur.

We had tea out on the lawn, very 'English' with the silver my mother had brought out with her, and the cookie soon learned to produce delicious cakes and sandwiches. Often there would be tennis and the young men would turn up whenever they wanted to. There was another European estate on the other side of the railway, known as 'Johore Labis'. The manager of this was Harry Adamson, and he and his two assistants came too. It got dark around 6.30 p.m., but we sat outside talking and drinking, until driven in by the mosquitoes. Even here the lights would attract vast hordes of flying beetles and other insects all intent on beating or burning themselves to death. Really, no one was completely safe from them, despite the various joss-stick burners and Flit pumps, until in bed under the mosquito net. One of our terrors was the bats. They got a hysterical welcome, and we would hold on to our hair while Charles, with a good many oaths, attempted to hit them down with a tennis racquet.

The nights were glorious. Often when the moon was up, I would lean over the verandah rail outside the bedroom. Everything would be bathed in a white magical light as clear as daylight, and the silence was filled with the high-pitched voices of thousands of tiny insects, but one became so used to this that one hardly heard them, and the noise became part of the background. If there were creatures prowling around, they kept hidden. There were mongooses in the roof, and occasionally they could be heard scuttling around, but they were encouraged, as they killed snakes and other undesirable creatures. There were nights when the coolies would be beating it up, literally, with tom-toms, but these were silenced at 10.00 p.m. and nothing further was heard from their quarters.

When it rained the bullfrogs would keep up their incessant croaking all night, which was distracting, but nothing compared with the nightjar which is reputed to send people insane. The Malays bet on this bird as its 'cloc cloc' was seldom consistent. It would cloc any number of times from one to seven, and one instinctively began counting. But to me, another sound was infinitely more upsetting. This was Joan having a nightmare and screaming the house down. We shared a room, and I would suddenly be woken by her blood-curdling screams and yells that there were monkeys on top of her mosquito net, or some such thing, and no amount of my shouting back that there was nothing there and not to be stupid, would pacify her. So I would sit up in bed hugging my knees waiting for the sound of our mother hastening down the verandah, hurricane lamp in hand, to the rescue. Joan would then wake up, but it took some time to console her and convince her that it had all been a dream.

All our visitors had to be warned, as the screams could be heard even as far as the boys' quarters at the back. They were all very intrigued and would question me, saying, 'Missie sister very sick last night?' But when I explained as well as I could that it was only bad dreams she was having, they apparently accepted this with wise nods, as the Chinese put tremendous significance into dreams.

I spent a lot of time at the 'back' talking to the 'boys' and we soon understood one another fairly well in Malay. I was also able to communicate to the *podiuns* in this, as they could speak it a little, and it was a far easier language than Tamil. There was a story Charles told, that when God finished making the World he was told all was completed except one thing, and that was the Tamil language. So he put some stones into a tin box and rattled it and said that will do for that, and it certainly did not sound unlike it.

These small boys who came up to the house to ball-boy were eventually allowed to come up and play with me, on other evenings, and I taught them any game I knew and then how to sing in English. They were very quick on the uptake and thought it was all a hugh joke. We organised a concert party with the family, assistants and boys as audience. The stage was between the vast poles that held up my swing and the whole thing caused some amusement both sides of the curtain. They giggled even more than my girl friends at home, no doubt partly from embarrassment, and because, obviously, they looked upon me as being a bit of an oddity.

I WAS ALWAYS WANTING TO HAVE a collection of animals, so I was delighted when an Indian who owed Charles money brought me a present of a little brown monkey. I was warned that it was not used to white people, so to be a bit careful to start with. I would steel myself to remain still while it climbed up my legs and put its arm round my neck in what I hoped was a show of love. But it obviously had other ideas and would grab hold of my cheek with one hand in order to give it a good bite, so instinctively I would throw it off and run. It was on a chain attached to a harness round its middle so could not attack me if I kept out of reach. All the same, I was very worried that I could not tame it despite the hundreds of bananas I tried bribing it with. In the end this proved to be its undoing, as it was found dead one morning, lying on its back with a huge extended stomach.

I felt bad about the whole affair, but was soon comforted by something else which became the real 'love of my life', apart from Pups. Charles had a great friend called Charles Renshaw. He lived a lonely life on a remote estate north of Labis, so he often caught the train to spend a weekend with us. I adored him as he was gentle, kind and generous and always showed a lot of interest in anything I did. After hearing the sad story of the monkey he asked me what animal I would most like to own. Of course this was a pony, and I could hardly believe it when a few weeks later he wrote to say there was one on the way.

I was in ecstasy when Charles and I went down to the station to meet her. She turned out to be a beautiful small, black, Delhi pony, a breed that have Arab blood in them, with a long mane and a tail sweeping the ground. I had only ridden a little, so Charles found an old retired Malay jockey living in the village who agreed to come up each day and teach me. He was quite a character and full of stories about his life on the track, but a good teacher apart from expecting me to ride with my knees practically touching my chin. I was soon able to cope on my own, and after that only saw him occasionally to wave to as I rode through the village. So from then on the syce and I looked after her, and Charles had a little stable built in the garden as we thought she was better there than down by the office where the old horse and the syce lived.

There were miles of road and tracks to ride through on the estate, and after a bit I was allowed to go through the village and along the new road that was being built from Labis to Bekok and which would eventually connect us with the outside world. There was also a track that led to a Malay *kampong* or village. I liked riding up there as the houses were all thatched and built high off the ground on stilts. The land was open paddy fields, where they cultivated their rice, and I much preferred this to the endless rows of rubber trees with which we were surrounded. Also the Malays were so friendly, saluting me with '*Tabi* Missie'

(Goodday Missie) and according to Charles, they were the 'gentlemen of the East'. They wore bright coloured clothes and were good looking, although the women seemed to grow old at a very early age. This was not surprising as they did most of the work. The men thought they had had a hard day if they spent it lying in the shade of one of the little huts built out on the paddy fields with a string attached to their big toes. When wiggled this rang a bell and frightened the birds away. Admittedly at harvest time everyone helped, including the children.

When I first went out riding on the estate, all the Tamil children would rush out and follow me. I would canter round the football field, showing off a bit, while they ran screaming and laughing after me and loving it if I turned suddenly and charged into the midst of them.

Sometimes I would visit the temple which was situated up a side road about a mile further on. This was for all the estate workers, who were Hindus and had brought their own God who was made of solid gold and was about two feet high. He was known by everyone as 'Sammy' and represented the God Shiva. The temple was looked after by two Tamil priests, who welcomed me with bows and invitations to go inside. So tethering the pony and taking off my boots, I would *Salaam* (greetings) Sammy who sat smugly smiling, surrounded by flowers, usually tuber-roses and gardenias with their sickly sweet smell. After a few moments I would touch my forehead with two hands and retreat backwards from his presence. Charles had demonstrated this correct behaviour the first time he had taken me there, and so I was accepted by the priests who would wave me goodbye and invite me to come back again soon.

Poor Sammy was only allowed out once a year when he was taken round the estate on the feast of Devali. After celebrating most of the day the men would be rather the worse for drink, and with a lot of singing and chanting they would bring him up to the bungalow, held high on a sort of platform affair by some of the elders. We would line up by the front entrance to be garlanded and the head priest would say a few words which Charles replied to. They would then return to the temple, and the others would go back to the 'Toddy' shop. This drink was made out of rice and coconut milk and was very potent.

The chief attraction of the week was the Sunday morning bathe. Charles had constructed a lovely pool out of a natural jungle waterfall and stream. It meant going in the dog-cart about two miles to the edge of the jungle, and then walking 300 yards or so down a track to the pool. The assistants would come too,

and we were quite pleased to have them, as the track was through wild virgin jungle. There were plenty of tigers about, but everyone assured us they never appeared during the heat of the day. The atmosphere was so casual and carefree, it was easy to forget any danger. The water was marvellously cool and we could not wait to plunge in after the hot walk, revelling in the crystal clear water and lying under the waterfall. The rest of the pool was quite large with dug-out canoes on it. These Charles had had made by some Chinese who were given permission to fell timber in an area nearby.

It was hard to drag oneself away when it was time to return for a late lunch, and I would be worried to death by the dogs who would go off hunting monkeys. Charles refused to wait for them more than a few minutes of frantic whistling, and so if they failed to return we would leave, me near to tears at the thought of them being torn to bits by a gang of monkeys, or perhaps, even worse, the tigers who must be lying up in some shady spot. But they always DID arrive back at the bungalow eventually, desperately hot and tired, but at least all in one piece.

We had quite a lot of visitors, one of them being our Irish doctor. He was only five feet tall and just as broad, and his wife was exactly the same shape, so they were known as Tweedledee and Tweedledum. They would usually both arrive by the morning train, jolly and perspiring, with a fund of gossip which Mrs Hicky was left to regale Mummy with, while he and Charles went off to the hospital. They had no children, and so she would annoy my mother by telling her what a grave mistake she had made in bringing me out to Malaya. 'At this age, Nina dear,' I would hear her saying, though supposedly engrossed in my lessons, 'you can't be too careful. Whatever you do, don't allow her to go anywhere on her own.' Luckily for me Mummy and Charles ignored this advice, and although I secretly thought her a silly old fool, I longed to know what ghastly fate she thought was in store for me. Some children were sent to a school up in one of the hill stations, but most of them went home at the age of six or seven.

Sometimes the Sultan of Johore would arrive with his retainers, to go into the jungle big game hunting after tiger or elephant, wild buffalo and rhino. He was a big man as a result of some European blood, and had the reputation of being very brave and a good shot. He tracked everything on foot, scorning the safe seat on top of a tame elephant. He had a Scottish wife, but also numerous Malay ones, and between them was supposed to have produced eighty children. Charles was a personal friend and a member of his council in Johore Bahru, the capital. For this he was given an honorary title, and when he had to attend meetings it was a good excuse for us all to get down to Singapore, only another seventeen miles further south.

The Sultan had a passion for the mangoes produced by a large tree in the garden, maintaining they were the best fruit in the country, so when it was in fruit he was given a vast basket of them when he departed. It hurt us to see so many go, as we agreed with him and loved to eat them ourselves. Still, like most fruit trees in Malaya, it fruited twice a year and gave a tremendous yield. They were messy fruit to eat, with masses of juice which ran down one's chin, and many people maintained that the only proper place to eat them was in the bath. I liked mangosteens almost better. They were quite different, with a tough red skin and lots of white sections inside exactly corresponding in number to the notches marked on the outside skin, and what a marvellous flavour.

Of course, according to the Malays, the finest fruit of all was the dorian. This was as large as a football, with a prickly skin and a really terrible smell. You were told to hold your nose when you first tasted one, and then the flavour was meant to be so exquisite you forgot the smell. The Malays also considered it an aphrodisiac which added to its attraction, and so during the fruiting season, luckily very short, very little work was done and the days and nights were spent in feasting. It was like a drug, and certainly the birth-rate was said to go up.

Another visitor, who was always more than welcome, was a French RC priest who came primarily to convert the heathens in our midst. He would appear always in good time for lunch and, full of charm, would kiss our hands, much to my embarrassment, and settle down to a hearty meal, during which he discussed world affairs in a light-hearted way, accompanied by roars of laughter.

He had a fund of stories, too, which after a couple of glasses of brandy became very amusing, and we were always sorry when he finally departed to see his small 'flock'. He would go swinging down the drive in his black boots, cassock flying, and shouting last farewells over his shoulder. We became very fond of him and wished his visits were more frequent.

It was a great event when we went visiting ourselves; we would catch the mid-day train to 'Segamat' or 'Batu Anam' where the

Hickeys lived. Both places had golf and tennis clubs, so people from all the surrounding estates would come to them in the evening. We felt we were in the world again and it was all very friendly and jolly, but there were only a few very young children. I was allowed to stay up for dinner parties, usually held in someone's house, and often returned to the club afterwards to dance to the gramophone. But I was a good excuse for Mummy and Charles to be the first to leave, as neither of them liked late nights and some of these parties went on to dawn. Joan would stay on out of politeness to the Hickeys, but she was really rather bored with the proceedings and attentions of various men who hoped she might forget John for a while.

One Sunday, on a beautiful moonlit night when one could see as clear as day, Dr Hickey suggested we all go for a drive to try and see a black panther which had been reported several times walking on a jungle road not far away. So after dinner we all piled into his big open car, the three women behind and he, Charles and me in front. Suddenly, right in the centre of the road we could see a large animal with its eyes shining in the headlights. When we were nearly on top of it, it began running in front of the car with its tail almost touching the driver's seat. I was terrified and quickly got over into the back. By this time the car was in an uproar with everyone shouting advice.

All the commotion apparently frightened the animal and it jumped to the side and disappeared into the jungle. Charles had to restrain the doctor from leaping out of the car and following it, armed with only a pistol which he always kept in the car for emergencies. 'Don't be such a hot headed fool,' shouted Charles, while the women were all for removing ourselves from the area as soon as possible. Once we were on the way back it was decided it had been quite an adventure. Even Charles, who had spent nights at Labis sitting up in a tree to try and shoot a tiger which had been meandering round the estate terrifying the tappers, had never seen any animal at such close quarters.

John turned up most weekends and Joan would go off with Charles to meet him off the night mail. So that she could greet him in private, it was Charles's habit to leave the car on the down side of the line, and Joan would be escorted over the level crossing to the station by 'Mabel' carrying a lantern. One night someone in the crowd grabbed hold of her, but her screams soon brought Charles running and by the time he reached her, Mabel and one or two others had chased her assailant off, but without catching him. No real harm was done, but Joan was very frightened and upset. By this time the train had come in, so she was able to fall into John's arms and be comforted. After this Charles always accompanied her, but it was the only unpleasant incident that occurred during all our time at Labis.

Joan and John spent the hours between lunch and tea lying on long chairs, holding hands and talking. I would hang around, and in order to get rid of me they were always sending me off on errands and little jobs. John invented things like packing, or putting in his cuff links, which anyway I rather enjoyed.

Fred Ward told us he hoped to get married when he went home on leave, and when we asked who to, he replied, 'I don't know yet, I've got to find her first'. Apparently he bought the ring on his way home in Colombo, where stones were cheap, and long afterwards his wife told Mummy how hurt she had been when she found out he had got it in anticipation, and was therefore obviously determined to marry *someone.* It must have been very lonely for them, although it was the accepted thing that they all had a Malay or Tamil girl to 'look after them'. Because of this Mummy was adamant that I did not visit any of them when I was out on my own, unless especially invited the day before. Naturally I did not know the reason, and thought her unnecessarily fussy.

Charles had pipe tobacco sent out from Dunhills in London. Three different kinds which had to be mixed up together and put into airtight tins to keep out the damp. I enjoyed this job, especially as I was able to keep a bit back for myself. I would retreat to my bamboo hut at the bottom of the garden, which the gardener had helped me build, and smoke this very strong mixture in a clay pipe which I bought in the village. Extraordinary to relate, I do not remember being sick.

THE HIGHLIGHT IN OUR LIVES was going down to Singapore when Charles had to attend one of the council meetings in 'Johore Bahru' which was only seventeen miles to the north and across the causeway over the Johore Straits that divided Singapore Island from the mainland. We stayed at the Europe Hotel, an old colonial style building beautifully situated overlooking the cricket ground and the harbour. The bedrooms were huge, and Charles thought the food and service better than at Raffles where we had spent our first memorable nights. It had no outside dining-room, but the grill-room, where we lunched, was noted for its shellfish and whitebait. Joan would be thrilled at seeing John every day, and we all loved the fascinating shops and the general air of life and bustle. All day there would be the continuous sound of the squeeze-horns on the taxis and cars; the drivers apparently thought full-time blowing essential to avoid an accident in the milling streets and roads. There were rickshaws everywhere, and people walked and ran across the roads without a glance, so it was rather a nerve-wracking business to drive or be driven.

There were thousands of interesting things to do. The shops, run mostly by Chinese and Indians, were full of exotic merchandise, mostly very cheap, and lots of the best ones were situated in the High Street, just at the side of the hotel. It was fun to buy Christmas presents to send home, knowing they would be unique, as it was before the days when the cheaper goods from the East were imported to Europe. North Bridge Road, not far away, was the street of the shoemakers. Here one could be fitted for a pair of shoes and collect them the next day. It was the same with the tailors and dressmakers, who were so good at faithfully copying a garment brought to them, that it was said they would even include a patch if it was there.

Sometimes after tea we went to the botanical gardens. There were lots of monkeys here, roaming free and continuously fed by the visitors so they had become very tame and cheeky. One of them pinched Mummy's handbag out of the back of the open car and swarmed up a tree with it. Luckily the clasp was too stiff to open so eventually it was dropped in disgust.

Quite often John took us to the Yacht Club which was down by the inner harbour, and Joan and I would go out sailing with him and his great friend, Ned Holiday, who owned a boat. There were races on Sunday and sometimes Ned would let us act as his crew. This was a great thrill, except when we got becalmed and had to wait for hours in the sun for a breeze to get up. Ned thought it very ignominious to accept a tow, except as a last resort. Once we turned over on our side and were thrown into the sea. We were still in the harbour where there were numerous sharks, and John upset Joan by asking her if she still had her engagement ring; she thought his main concern should have been our safety. We later found out one could walk on the sails, as these boats never turn right over.

Sometimes we had dinner in one of the Japanese restaurants. I always thought what fun it would be to live in one, as they were built on stilts over the sea and were reached along a platform. We sat on the matted floor while a friendly, sweet looking little woman squatted in the middle of us, cooking on a small stove let into a low table. It was a sort of stew made of meat or chicken and very young vegetables, served with rice and soya bean sauce. It was delicious, and doubly attractive because of the friendly atmosphere and being completely surrounded by sea, often with a moon making a path across the water. Later, some friends of Joan and John's, Joan and Maurice Yates, made my dream come true by buying up one of these restaurants which was closing and converting it into an enchanting house.

There were plans in the air for the wedding which was going to take place early the next year. Mummy and Joan bought a lot of the lovely materials in the native shops, and back on the estate spent many hours converting them into underclothes for the trousseau. My mother would also pay a visit to 'John Little's' where she would buy quantities of imported edible goods to put in the store cupboard. Tins of fruit and vegetables, chocolates and sweets, were all packed in a large hamper to take back with us. When it was time to return to Labis, John would drive us to the station about 6.00 p.m. when the night mail left for Johore. The journey took four hours and was mostly in the dark. The monotony was relieved when about halfway, at a small station called Kluang, the boys from the rest-house there would bring us down a hot dinner, beautifully packed in a special tin container consisting of four separate compartments fitting neatly on top of one another. It kept the food, which never varied, piping hot; fried fish, roast chicken and vegetables and tinned peaches and cream, which was my idea of a perfect meal. This helped to pass the time, and afterwards we would play cards until at last we stopped at Labis and staggered sleepily into the waiting dogcart.

Next day we would unpack the stores into the large cupboard of which Mummy kept the key. This was not because the boys were not trusted, but because they would not have been able to resist using them all up in the first few days. There was good local meat and chickens, but most of the fish and vegetables would be sent packed in ice down from Kuala Lumpur. There were plenty of locally grown vegetables, but they were not altogether safe to eat as the methods of growing them were not too sanitary and could result in dysentery. Instead of a refrigerator, there was a large ice box which was replenished with ice from the village each day. The boy would mix fresh lime and keep it in bottles on the ice, and this was the best soft drink I ever tasted. These limes were also the basis for the 'gin slings' Charles always made after bathing on Sundays.

Charles decided the horse was getting too old, so he pensioned it and the syce off, and bought a car. He had never driven before, but quite undaunted, and rather like Toad of Toad Hall, he soon mastered the elementaries and careered round the estate to the terror of any other traffic. Admittedly this did not amount to more than a few bullock carts, who hastily removed themselves into the nearest ditch, or one of the assistants on a motorbike. It was all taken pretty light-heartedly, and Charles, full of confidence by then, suggested both Mummy and Joan had a go. My mother showed remarkably little aptitude or enthusiasm and soon gave up altogether, and Joan nearly ended in disaster by driving right through the garage which was made of wood, so the end wall collapsed like a pack of cards. There was a steep bank beyond but she managed to put on the brakes without going over the edge. This unnerved her, but the final straw was when she wrenched off one of the car doors on the garage door as I was trying to open it, nearly knocking me down at the same time. So Charles was the only driver when we ventured forth into the outer world. He must have been a brave man, and we too as his passengers.

We were to set out on a 150 mile journey for a holiday at Port Dickson, which was over on the west coast. This was an adventure which was to take us quite a while to get over. It started one early morning with the car being hoisted into a specially ordered truck on the goods train that went through Labis daily at 6.30 a.m. We travelled in the guard's van and disembarked at the next station, eight miles up the line. This was the start of the road which would eventually join up with Labis. After a lot of palaver with the station master and the usual crowd that had gathered to watch the proceedings and stand open-mouthed at the sight of us and the luggage being fitted into the car, we were ready to start. Mummy and Charles were in front and Joan and I in the back.

The car was an open Maxwell with a canvas roof which kept

the sun off but not the red dust from the laterite roads. By the time we stopped for lunch at the rest-house, we had already had two punctures. Charles, of course, had never changed a wheel in his life, and had no intention of trying in the heat, but luckily the first time it happened we were near a village where a Chinese garage of sorts was capable of doing the job. Further on a passing taxi man obliged. As we ate our lunch someone in the village came to the rescue, so we set off again, like the typical 'mad dogs and Englishmen', in the extreme heat of the afternoon. The road led between rubber trees and jungle, and the lovely open paddy fields and attractive Malay villages, which became more numerous as we got nearer the coast.

There were lots of wooden bridges over quite large rivers, and here all the smaller children who were not in school would be bathing, the boys stark naked, while their sisters, some of them quite beautiful, and mothers would be doing the family wash well covered by their wet sarongs tucked under their armpits. The children were very excited at seeing us go by, and waved and shouted greetings, but the women were shy and giggling, turned their heads away. It intrigued us the way they used their sarongs as a sort of tent when they were bathing, bobbing up and down inside them, with their waist-length hair floating out around them, and looking very attractive. When they came out they tucked their sarongs very efficiently above their busts and with seemingly one twist knotted their hair into a bun at the nape of their necks. No pins were used, and it seldom seemed to come down.

We really thought our last hour had come when halfway up a steep hill the car started to go backwards. Charles, letting forth a good many oaths, miraculously steered us down to the bottom without going into the ditch. Joan and I clung to each other, offering up silent prayers, but Mummy remained calm and apparently unmoved, although it was a bit nerve-racking realising we had got to make the attempt a second time. Still, with a good many yells from the back, and grinding of gears from Charles, we eventually got up.

The traffic on the roads consisted of an occasional taxi, bicycles and motor bikes, and once or twice a private car with a European in it. These automatically stopped to have a word with us, whether we had met before or not. Most of the planters knew each other by reputation, and were only too pleased to see a new face and give a little local advice. The two we met were horrified at our tales of woe, and although at a loss to know how to assist us, at least helped to boost our morale, and we continued buoyed up with their good wishes for better luck for the rest of the way. We passed several little boys leading the huge water buffalos the Malays use for ploughing and hauling. These look extremely fierce and were reputed to dislike white people, but in the hands of the smallest Malay boy, they were quite biddable. When not being worked they spent their time wallowing in the muddy water down the sides of the rice fields, with only their heads emerging.

Suddenly, about halfway on the final lap and about fifteen miles from our destination, when we were all thinking of the delights of baths and cool drinks, there came that ominous grinding sound which could only mean another puncture. Charles decided to carry on and there really was not much option, short of spending the night where we were, as the spare tyre had not been mended, so on we bumped. It was dark by now, but after what seemed like eternal jungle we could just make out an open space to our left which, to our joy, turned out to be the sea glimpsed through coconut trees, and reflections on the water from the oil lamps came from the Malay huts built right down on the edge of the sandy beaches. At last we came to several large bungalows set in gardens amidst casuarina trees, the attractive feathery pine that grows in the sand. The Chinese staff who rushed out to greet us had nearly given us up for lost as it was nearly 9.30 p.m. by this time, but they soon had everything in working order, turning up the cheerful oil lamps, unpacking the car and bringing iced drinks while we washed, and finally a very good dinner, after which we all fell into bed exhausted.

WE WOKE THE NEXT MORNING to enchanted surroundings, eating breakfast on a verandah that overlooked a large white sandy bay and calm blue sea only fifty yards away. The bathing was perfect, a gentle shelving beach to deep water where a diving platform was built, and warm enough to stay in all day. It was more refreshing early in the morning or late in the evening, as at mid-day it could feel like a hot bath. There was no danger from sharks but one saw an occasional jellyfish, easy enough to avoid in the clear water. The main occupation of the Malays was fishing, and their boats lined the beach. These were known as *kolehs* and were very light with no outrigger to steady them. In the stiff breeze that often got up with the high tide, the Malays had to lean out so far they appeared to be sitting in the sea. During their weekends – the Malay Sunday was on Friday – they held *koleh* races, two men handling the frail looking little boats and making them fly along even with very little wind.

The women had an industry of their own. They would come along the beach, when we were sitting under the trees after bathing, with huge baskets balanced on their heads. They would put these down at our feet and out of them produce masses of smaller ones, all shapes and sizes. They were shy of us at first, giggling at our attempts at bargaining, but approving all the same as it was all part of the game. Lots of the women were quite old and very inquisitive, asking Charles lots of personal questions about our ages and relationships to him. We bought quite a lot from them as the baskets were absurdly cheap, and although fairly roughly finished off, were simple and in bright attractive colours as well as in natural straw. In fact we became so friendly it was difficult to avoid a daily purchase, but after a time they came just to talk and to examine us in detail at close range. They were apparently fascinated by my long fair hair, picking it up if I gave them a chance and even touching my face to make sure the pink and white did not come off. Being brown skinned themselves, they were the opposite to us who were trying hard to get a sun tan. They admired a pale complexion and would often ruin their looks, when they dressed up to go somewhere, by using almost white powder. It was impossible to take offence at their friendly advances, especially as they had a great sense of humour and laughed uproariously at our simple jokes which were translated by Charles if our miming was too difficult for them.

Poor Joan had an accident soon after our arrival and was not allowed by the doctor to bathe again. Her foot was terribly badly cut on the barnacles that clung below the water line on the diving platform. Luckily John was coming up to join us. He appeared a few days later, having caught the train to Seramban, a town on the railway line about thirty miles from Port Dickson, and from there had hired a taxi. Joan was quite happy to spend most of the day with him under the casuarina trees. The sun was so powerful that it was possible to get quite badly burned even when bathing and apparently covered most of the time by water. I became very pink for the first few days, but soon had a coating of brown which protected me.

Port Dickson village was only six or seven miles away, so we occasionally went there to shop. It was very attractive with beautiful old flame of the forest trees lining the streets. These were covered by great clusters of red flowers. The shops were owned by Chinese and Malays who sold, among other things, the gaily coloured sarongs they wore. These were in hand blocked cotton and silk, woven and made on the spot, but most of the silk ones came from the East Coast. There was a happy relaxed atmosphere, and one was welcomed everywhere. Nobody was ever in a hurry and you felt everyone had the leisure to enjoy life.

From the bungalow it was possible to walk along the sands in both directions for some way. When the tide was out the Malay women would be out looking for mussels and crabs in the pools, and there was a great variety of shells to be found. My mother loved the sea and often felt very cooped up on the estate, but I never heard her complain, although it must have taken a lot of courage to accept the complete change from the life she had lived in London. Obviously she missed my brother a great deal and worried about his future.

I often thought back to the night in London when she had first told us that she was going to marry again, and so change the whole pattern of our lives. The door had burst open into the bedroom Joan and I shared, and to our astonishment there was Mummy looking flushed and quite unlike her usual calm self. It all came out in a rush. She was going to marry Charles, and we were all three going back to Malaya with him and she hoped we were as excited at the prospect as she was. I was astounded; although I liked Charles very much, it had not occurred to me to think of him as a possible stepfather. As the idea began to sink in, I was horrified at the thought of leaving all the familiar things, my school, my friends and particularly my beloved brother. 'What will happen to Jack?' I wailed, by then working myself into a state.

Poor Mummy, I could see I had touched her on the raw here. She tried to explain that she was upset at the thought of leaving him as she knew he would be, but after all he was only sixteen and must finish his education at Malvern. Joan was just nineteen and I was nine years younger. She at least responded magnificently. She threw her arms round Mummy's neck, saying how pleased she was for her, and how thrilled she was at the thought of leaving London and the excitement of the voyage and visiting so many foreign places on the way. After Mummy left us, she tried to talk me round to the idea that it was all going to be a great adventure, and finally I went to sleep a little happier about it all.

But the next morning I could not help worrying about Jack. He was a wonderful brother and I adored him. During the holidays he took me out around London. We sailed model boats on the Round Pond, visited the zoo and the museums, and played an exciting game he made up of pretending we were detectives. We chose some innocent but interesting looking person out of the crowds, and then tried to follow him. This led us into various peculiar places, and often left us standing out in a street miles from home when the person disappeared into a house, slamming the door behind him and still quite oblivious of our sleuthing. We also spent a part of our holidays in the country with our Gabriel cousins, whose mother was our mother's elder sister.

We loved it there, though we were all a bit frightened of Uncle Chris. He was a very big man with a large moustache, with an addiction to dressing in rather loud checks. He always wore a carnation in his buttonhole, which was put in a little lalique vase in the hall each morning by the head gardener, and after breakfast he would disappear in a chauffeur driven car to Woking station where he caught the train to London. We felt more at home with my Aunt Elsie, and she never interfered with our days as long as we turned up at the right time for meals. There was plenty to do, as apart from masses of dogs, there were horses, a farm and a huge garden with a pavilion with every sort of gadget including a ping-pong table, parallel bars and even fencing outfits. There were two boys, John and Ralph, a little older than me, and an older girl and boy, so Jack would at least have them to spend his holidays with, which was some comfort.

When I told my friends where I was going, they all thought I was in tremendous luck, getting away from school in particular, and they pictured my swinging in jungle trees like Jane of Tarzan fame, the current favourite. This all helped to quell my doubts and I became affected by the general excitement and all the bustle of selling the house, and of packing up china, silver and glass, and even bits of furniture to be shipped out with us. Our dear Clara, who had looked after us all since my father died and my Nannie had gone off to get married, tried to keep up a cheerful facade but really the bottom was dropping out of her world. She adored my mother and several times I found her brushing tears away which of course then started me off, but she would pull us both together by saying, 'Enough of this nonsense,' and we would soon be laughing a little hysterically at one of her many jokes. She was a marvellous woman, and I never remember her in anything but a good temper.

We must have tried her to the limit at times too, creeping downstairs and ringing the front door bell, getting her flying down the three storeys from the kitchen, which was at the top of the house, only to find no one there. But she never let on that she knew it was us, muttering away to herself about all the people she suspected, and we really believed she did not know. Even when we made bloodcurdling noises hiding in a cupboard or under the kitchen table, she would pretend to faint into the old basket armchair while we crept from the room and then she would appear groaning and ask us to look for the culprits.

When the time at last arrived for us to catch the boat train down to the London docks to board the *City of Paris,* Clara and Jack came to see us off. There was a drama halfway to the station when Mummy discovered that her hatbox had been left behind. Poor Clara was put into another taxi to rush back and fetch it, and told to try and catch us up at the station. She only just made it, running for dear life down the platform, her little short legs flying and the tears beginning to flow. We pulled the box in through the window just as the whistle blew, no chance for any last minute hugs, and the train started to move leaving her and Jack supporting each other, and all of us trying to bravely wave through a mist of tears. We wept all the way down; poor Charles, what an ordeal for him. But we began to dry up and look about us with the excitement of the docks, and getting on board and finding our cabins, then exploring the ship.

The next three days plunged us into even greater misery. From the moment we got into the Bay of Biscay the ship started to roll, and the three of us never stopped throwing up. Charles must have wondered what he had let himself in for, but he behaved like a saint and, instead of leaving us to the stewardess, dashed between the two cabins like a ministering angel as we lay moaning and groaning on our bunks wishing we were dead. Few things can bring one to such a desperate low state of mind and body, but suddenly we were in calm waters sailing smoothly in the Mediterranean with the sun shining through the port-holes and beckoning us up on deck. We staggered upstairs, and the fresh air worked wonders. Within an hour I was feeling perfectly fit, but it took Mummy and Joan a little longer. They lay on deckchairs with their feet up, eating grapes and sipping fresh lemonade. Later on in the day, when they were feeling stronger, they were soon surrounded by acquaintances of Charles and various young men who edged in at the sight of a good looking girl.

There was a great dearth of these on board or, for that matter, anywhere in the Far East, so any girl with any pretence of beauty had a marvellous time. As for the children, there must have been at least fifty, all ages, mostly quite young. The few that were around my age were on their way to Shanghai where the climate was good and there were several schools. We soon knew each other well, and we had a wonderful time with the run of the ship and very little supervision. Some of the older passengers complained about us, particularly when we disturbed their afternoon sleep by playing hide and seek down the passages outside the cabins. But on the whole we were tolerated and spoilt by all the ship's officers. One of Joan's young men wrote a rhyme about me in my autograph book which I was not quite sure how to take:

What do you call a girl like Pam,
Who behaves like a mite and looks such a lamb,
She loves you at one o'clock, hates you at three
And bites you to death by afternoon tea.

But perhaps it was quite an insight on the average nine year-old under these circumstances.

Joan soon singled out two young men who were her constant companions, and I was often roped in to make a four at the various deck games. We also swam in the canvas pool erected on deck, and in the evenings there would be a band and they would dance on the deck under the stars, which I thought very romantic. It was a great excitement when we reached our second port of call. The first was Marseilles, where we took a car with friends along the 'Cornich Road' and ate marvellous food at a cafe. Then it was Port Said. I simply adored the swarming jostling crowds of Arabs and Egyptians in the narrow streets, all trying to sell us something and calling Charles 'Captain'. He, we gathered, did not share our opinion and said they were all a lot of thieving bastards. Then came Aden, very hot and dry, but we much preferred the comparative calm of Colombo. It certainly was beautiful, with a lovely coastline, and we spent a day at Mount Lavinia with its sandy beach shaded by coconut trees. Back on board and headed now on the last lap to Singapore, it became obvious to everyone that Joan had fallen in love with one of her young men. This was John Cutler.

So here he was in Port Dickson making plans with Joan for their future, but very sweetly they included me in them all, so I would not feel left out, assuring me that once they were married and living in Singapore, I could go and stay with them as often as I liked, and Mummy and lessons could spare me. We hated to have to leave such a heavenly place, but I was eager to see the dogs and pony again, and vastly relieved to have John with us for the return journey. We were a bit squashed in the back but it was well worth it, and everything went much better with only two punctures, both at convenient places. Charles allowed John to drive some of the way, so he was able to sit back a bit, but obviously quite unable to relax, as like a lot of drivers he had little faith in anyone but himself.

WHEN WE GOT BACK to a rapturous welcome from the dogs, there was a letter to say there was another dog on its way from England. This was a belated wedding present sent by a friend of my mother's who bred fox-terriers. His name was Nigger, and he was smaller than the other two and had not got the same kind temperament. But I soon discovered he was easy to teach and he could do tricks, and to my amazement took to riding on the bar of my bicycle as if born to it. The first time he jumped up as if asking to be lifted on. I picked him up and his front paws went over the handlebars, and his back legs crossed themselves under the bar. I could not believe my eyes, he was so sure of himself, and never looked like falling. After a bit I always took him about with me like this, though I did tie a little cushion on to the bar, after Mummy had pointed out that after all he was a boy and therefore might find the bar a bit uncomfortable.

At the same time as this we got the news that Harry Adamson, who was home on leave, had followed Charles's example and had married a widow with a son of nine, and they would all be arriving quite soon. The boy, whose name was John Simpson, was only to stay out six months before returning home to a prep. school. I was quite thrilled at the thought of having a companion of more or less my own age. I was used to boys although my two 'Gabriel' cousins were both older than me, and this John was year younger.

As it happens both he and his mother turned out to be a disappointment to us all. Mrs Adamson was a good-looking woman of about thirty-five, but she had a bad-tempered expression, and apparently disapproved of nearly everything, including the way I was brought up. 'You're far too soft with her,' she would tell my mother in my hearing, 'What she needs is a good hiding like I give John when he is cheeky and disobedient.' Poor John in the consequences looked terrified most of the time. He was very thin and timid, and if I tried to egg him on to something, he would go running to his mother complaining I was a bully. I expect I was, but I was not going to have my world ruined, and so told him he was soft and if he was

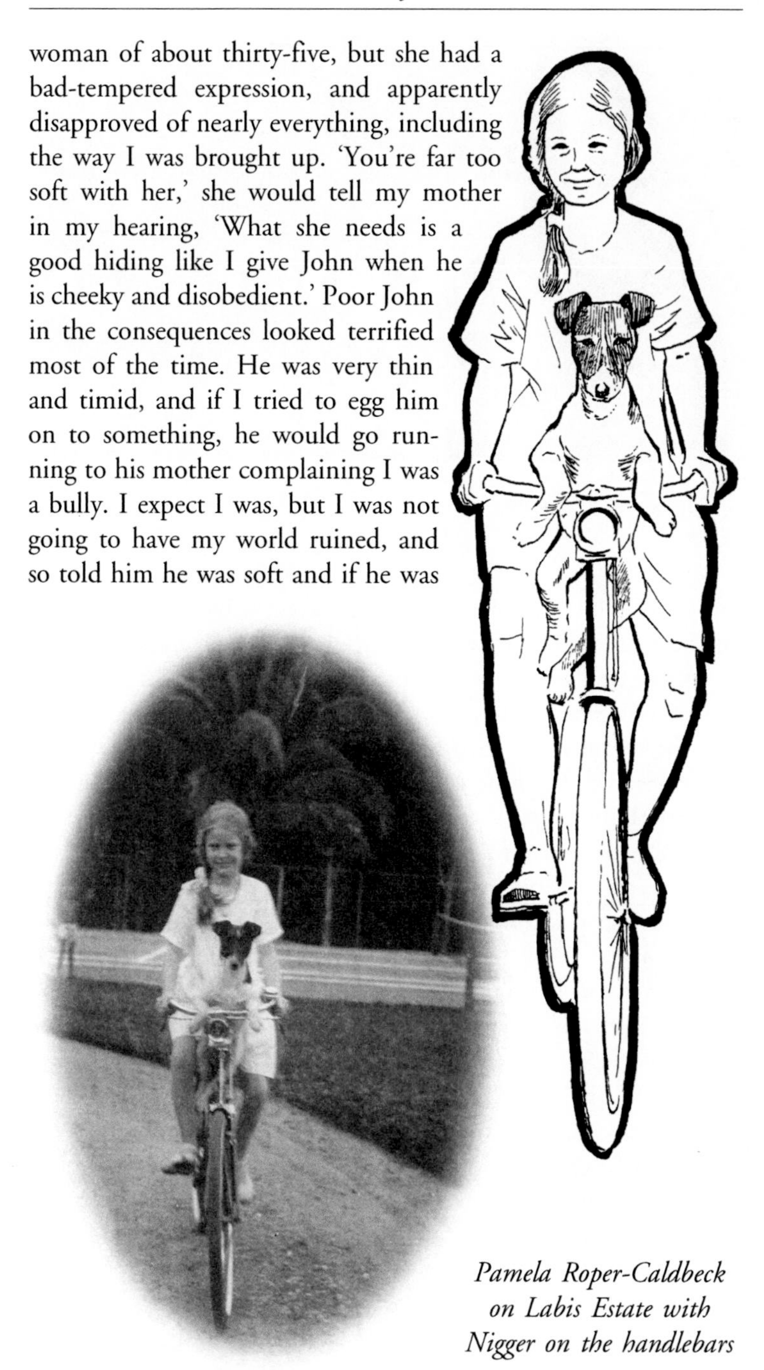

Pamela Roper-Caldbeck on Labis Estate with Nigger on the handlebars

Mother, Charles and the author (with Nigger on her lap) at Labis Estate

going to fit into the life he had better get a bit tougher. With this he replied that anyway he despised girls, and indicated that it was practically a fate worse than death having to associate with one, so our relationship was not exactly a happy one.

Both Mummy and Joan found Mrs Adamson equally difficult as she spent all the time complaining of the heat and the life in general. All the assistants loathed her. So we were all vastly relieved when she departed to take John back to school. She never returned, and although we felt sorry for Harry, he never talked about her, so perhaps he was secretly pleased at the way things turned out.

Mummy had her hair cut short on one of our trips to Singapore. We all felt very hot with long hair, so Joan and I soon decided to have ours cut too. John was very against Joan losing her tresses, but one day she begged Mummy to cut it off. By the time she had got halfway round her head, they were both weeping – I, who could not wait to get my own off, urged them not to be so silly and that the operation could not stop there – so Mummy finished it off and we consoled Joan by saying how much it suited her, and then it was my turn. Joan was worried stiff when Friday night arrived, what John would say? As it turned out he never even noticed until his attention was drawn to it by Joan, feeling thoroughly hurt at his being so unobservant.

TIME WAS DRAWING NEAR for the wedding, which was to be held in the cathedral in Singapore. I was to be the only bridesmaid and to wear a long dress of silver. I was not too happy about this, and felt more at home in jodhpurs or shorts, but Mummy and Joan assured me that I would look lovely. They were both in a mounting fever about it all, and our visits to Singapore became more and more frequent. The reception was to be held in the Europe, and they were going to Sumatra for their honeymoon. On one of these trips, instead of staying in Singapore, we went instead to Johore Bahru and stayed with friends of Charles's, the Gawlers. They lived in an old rambling house high up on a hill overlooking the Straits of Johore towards Singapore. The Gawlers had no children of their own, so made a great fuss of me. My mother became very fond of them both, so we all enjoyed being with them. We could go into Singapore to shop and get back before lunch, as it was only seventeen miles across the island to the City.

Johore Bahru was not a big town, but was very attractively laid out, with the Sultan's Palace and most of the European houses set back from the Straits, which were about a mile wide, among gardens with lovely old trees, and flowering shrubs, giving them park-like surroundings. After tea we would go down to the club which was on a level with the water. Here there would be a few European children playing, watched over by a group of Chinese nurse-maids or 'amahs', while their parents played golf or tennis, or just sat and gossiped. The amahs always managed to choose the dustiest spot and as near to the road as possible for their charges to play in, and here they would squat on their haunches, talking and laughing in their high-pitched strident voices, and yelling at any friend who passed by on the road. They were always spotless in their uniforms of black sateen trousers and white cotton blouses made with the high Chinese neck, with their long black hair, oiled smooth and shiny, pulled back into a bun, sometimes with a gold pin or two stuck in for decorations. They were kind and cheerful, but spoilt the children dreadfully, and most of their charges as a result treated their amahs with very little respect and did exactly as they wanted.

I would go down to play with them, but could not help despising the amahs' lack of authority and their sing-song English irritated me. 'Missie velly big girl,' they would say. 'Missie no want amah to cally for her.' I agreed whole-heartedly with this and wondered how true it was that they were supposed to give babies and even small children opium to make them sleep. Still, I suppose they were a Godsend to the mothers, and so cheap compared to an English 'Nannie'.

The week we were staying with the Gawlers happened to coincide with a garden party given by the Sultan, to which we were all invited. The palace was a large pink stone building with beautifully kept gardens. He had several sons who had been educated in England and who often attended these functions, but none of his Malay wives and daughters were allowed to appear. His European wife would be there, covered in huge diamonds and apparently quite at ease despite all the others peeping out of the windows. She had been married before to a Scottish doctor whom she had divorced in order to marry the Sultan, and they certainly seemed very happy in what, to her, must have been rather unusual circumstances.

The Gawlers took us to a Malay wedding which was held in a village only a few miles away. The bride had been in their employ and was now marrying a young man chosen by her parents. She had not even seen him before he was presented to her the week before the wedding, with both sets of parents and various relations present. They were not expected to talk to each other, and were lucky if they could even get in a good look. But apparently they were both quite happy about the arrangement and accepted it as the custom. She had brought a good dowry and he had a steady job driving for one of the estate managers, so what more could one ask for?

When we arrived we were taken to inspect them both. They were seated side by side on raised chairs in the house of the bride, and they were dressed in beautiful silk hand-embroidered clothes, with heavy gold headdresses. The bride's face was plastered with white powder and her eyes heavily kohled. Seeing them, one was hardly given the impression of a joyful occasion, but everyone else was obviously out to have a good time, and there was a great deal of laughing and shouting among the guests who all seemed pleased to see us and made us very welcome.

We were soon all seated at long low tables and plyed with every sort of curry which we ate off giant leaves with our fingers. This was washed down by beer and lemonade, and we finished up with some of the sweetest jellies and cakes I have ever tasted. There was also *gula malacca*, a sweet made from tapioca, with coconut milk and liquid brown sugar poured over it. This was meant to cool the mouth if the curry had proved a bit hot. Afterwards there was a 'ronhing', the Malay name for a dance. This consisted of various couples performing on a raised platform, erected for the occasion outside the house under the palm trees. The steps are quite intricate and raise a good deal of advice and merriment from the onlookers, as the main object is for the girl, who faces her partner, to entice him into touching her. If he does he is disqualified and another one takes his place.

All this time the poor bride and groom just sat there taking no part, and not being expected to talk or look at each other. They looked almost doped, but maybe they were just desperately nervous and tired, as this went on from early morning to night and, in some cases, for two or three days. At last the moment came for them to retire to the nuptial bed, which we had all been taken to inspect. A huge brass-knobbed double bed decked out in gorgeous bright colours, and with the hardest, highest and most uncomfortable looking pillows I have ever seen. This was a signal for our departure, but whether the couple ever got to bed without any onlookers seemed highly dubious. Joan remarked on the way back that it had been quite an experience, but she was quite pleased that our customs were rather different.

AT LAST THE TIME HAD ARRIVED for us to depart for the wedding. We had been back on the estate for about six weeks and Joan and Mummy were both feverishly working away to get everything ready in time. The actual wedding dress was being made at a shop in Singapore, so we had to go down there a few days before for a final fitting, etc. We stayed at the Europe, and finally the great day arrived. No one could eat any lunch and even after an attempt to get something down, we still had to wait some hours as it was too hot then, and therefore nobody was married before 4.00–5.00 p.m. Even so, it was hard not to spoil one's finery and we were continually wiping away the perspiration.

Mummy had a dress of black lace with long sleeves which must have been agony, but it looked very nice. Joan and I were both fairly cool with no sleeves, but *her* dress was only to the knees with a waist somewhere round her hips. This was the latest fashion from England, so the woman in the shop had told us, though I think Joan had a few secret doubts about the effect. Still, Mummy and I bolstered her up, saying how marvellous she looked, and she really did as she was pretty enough to overcome any style of dress. But she became more and more silent and nervous, and obviously it was all quite an ordeal for her. I was hot and embarrassed by my long dress and large flat silver shoes which pinched my toes. I was also terrified that I might trip over my skirt going up the aisle.

The wedding took place in the Cathedral and somehow we got through the ceremony without mishap and were able at last to relax in the vestry and walk down the aisle again to the strains of the famous march. I had a wonderful time at the reception and wallowed in all the attention I got. I danced with all the young men, talked too much, laughed too loudly, and generally behaved as if the champagne had gone to my head. It probably had, although I was officially only given one glass. Still, they did not allow me to get too big for my silver shoes, pulling my leg with 'poor girl she'll never be as beautiful as her sister', not that I was not always fully aware of this, because Charles and John never stopped telling me how big my mouth was, and that I had a nose like India rubber. Still what did I care? I was having the time of my life.

Pamela at Joan's wedding

At last the time came for Joan and John to depart for their honeymoon, amid tears, confetti and masses of tin cans as well as a rickshaw tied on to the back of their car. God knows how they got rid of it all, as I do not think anyone was sophisticated enough to have thought of a change of cars. When everyone had gone, we went rather sadly up to our rooms, but luckily someone had arranged a party at Raffles for which, as a special treat, I was to be allowed to stay up. This almost made up, anyway for the moment, for the realisation that Joan would not be there when we returned to the estate. There were sixteen of us at the party. I was given another glass of champagne, but I was already on the crest of a wave, buoyed up with too much attention, which had certainly by this time gone to my head. We ate under the stars by candlelight and a full moon, and danced until midnight. But suddenly it was all over and I fell into bed with the silver dress in a heap on the floor.

The next day we were down to earth with a bang, and returned to Labis. The dogs were so pleased to see us and danced round us as if we had been gone for years. I don't think dogs have any sense of time. Now that I had the vast bedroom to myself, I started to re-arrange it. It really was a large room with only one bed in it, but Charles got the estate carpenter to make me new bookshelves and another desk. Everyone went out of their way to be extra kind. The cookie told me he had some angora rabbits and would I like two. I was given a pair who like lightning produced a family. The hutch was kept under the famous mango tree, and one day to my horror I found the babies had been attacked by a particularly vicious type of red ant called a *karinga.* The poor little things had them clinging on to the skin all round their eyes. We picked them off, and removed the hutch and run to a large table on the verandah outside the dining-room. The table legs were stood in cups of disinfectant, the only sure way of keeping ants away, and this applied also to our own dining table. They, the rabbits, all survived, and I would take the whole family out on the lawn for an airing. They never ran away and the dogs took no notice of them.

Sometimes we were plagued by a swarm of ticks. These had to be seen to be believed. They would swarm into the bungalow, even upstairs, and once Mummy and I picked up as many as a hundred in five minutes. These we drowned in a large basin of water, then we used a Flit gun to finish off any lurking in the corners.

An old friend of my mother's turned up to stay at about this time. We liked her, but after a month were wondering if she would ever depart. Finally, she went off to Colombo to more friends and I wrote a letter to my 'old' Nannie after her going. This she gave me as one of her treasured possessions about forty years later. Here it is, spelling and all:

Darling Nannie.

You must be thinking me rather a wreket old sinner not answering your letter before, but we have been so busy writing to people about the wedding and I left you out as Mum has sent you a letter. Thank you for your letter. I love to get them and its very kind of you to write so often. I must wish you a happy Christmas and N. Year. Will you please give the little stuffed lizard to your son Ralph – I wish I could see him. The pink box is for you with every bit of love from me that you want. I am so pleased with life at the moment as Uncle Renshaw has given me a lovely little arab pony. I can ride her by meself now, and so far have only fallen off twice. I love riding. I ride astride and were breches which are very comfortbal – I can't spell that. The wedding was a great sucess and Joanie looked lovely, especially when she stood up at the alter with the sun shining on her hair and a slight breeze gently blowing her viel. I think I did every thing alright, thank goodness. I suppose you know my dress was silver tissue down to my feet, and I had a silver shoes and a pink wreath and posy of carnations, Joans going away dress was powder-blue with a deeper coloured cloche felt hat.
They had a great send off and there car was covered with paper streamers, and on the back was tied old tin cans and shoes etc; and to complete it they tied on with hankies and trailing out behind, a rickshaw. I felt sorry for the old chinaman it belonged to, but what could he do with heaps of Englishmen pushing him out of the way, and telling him to shut up. They came back from their honeymonn too weeks ago, they went to lake Tober in Sumatra, and now they are settling down in their house in S'pore. They had hundreds of wedding presents which help to make it look nice. When you write to her you address it like this – 'Mrs O. E. H. Cutler, Lewes & Peat, Singapore' that is Johns office address but everybody here seems to do that, for some reason or other. Now to answer your questions. Your son Ralph seems to be getting quite a scolar what with reading and writing, soon he wont have anything more to lern. Ha. Ha. Yes I heard from Mable, and she wrote to Mummie saying they had found a house and were to get married. There seem to be a lot of weddings as Uncle Renshaw had just got married, and Mr Ward who works on the

estate is going to soon, but she hasnt arrived, she is coming out from england. Now you say your two brothers are thinking of it too. Aunt Evie has been staying here, and then she went to columbo and now she's in Eastbourne and says she has'nt a sue left poor thing. Mummie has'nt heard from Emily for a year. I must ask these questions about Ralph and then go to bed. What time does HE go to bed and when is his birthday? With heaps of love and wishes for a merry christmas – how lucky you are to have it cold.

Please write again soon.
Love from Pamela.

P. S. Tell Ralph I have'nt seen any more wild animals recently.

There was always talk of snakes coming into the bungalow and finding their way up the drainpipes into the cool of the bathrooms. I found one weaving about on the water pipe above my bath and yelled for the Tukan Ayer, who soon dispatched it with a couple of blows with his wooden clogs, assuring me at the same time that it was only a grass snake and therefore not dangerous. But occasionally the gardener would shout up that he had seen a cobra, and Charles would get his gun and often shoot it from the verandah. One day the coolies brought a small brown bear they killed and set up in a kind of frame to present to us. We pretended to be impressed as they were wildly enthusiastic, but really we thought it rather pathetic-looking, and were sorry for it as they do not do any harm and it must have had a violent death.

Charles would go off, accompanied by two or three Chinese, for a whole day into the high jungle hills, looking for tin. There was definite proof of tin veins and he would bring back samples which they found, but there was never sufficient to make it worthwhile setting up a dredge. Sometimes it would be well after dark before he returned and my mother would start getting worried. When he did arrive, very hot and tired, he would be covered from head to foot with little red ticks and leeches. These had to be burned off with a lighted cigarette or the end of Charles's pipe as the nicotine made them drop their hold. If you pulled them with your fingers it made a really sore place. We all set to work on him including the head boy, and it would take us some time to free him of these parasites.

Soon after Joan and John came back from their honeymoon, we went down to Singapore to see them. John was full of stories about the wild men who lived in the hills around Prapat where they had stayed in a hotel, and on the vast island in Lake Tober the women were reputed to be killed off when they reached the age of sixty. Apparently one day they had gone for a walk and found themselves being followed by a villainous looking man holding a long carved knife. They were some way from the hotel, so started to walk very fast, and then broke into a run when John, on looking back, said he was gaining on them. But, eventually, as they neared the village, he disappeared.

Joan was so upset by all this that she had one of her nightmares and woke screaming that there was a man coming for her with a knife. Of course John believed her and playing the brave hero, he flung himself on top of her thinking to receive the knife instead. Of course this made matters worse as feeling she was being suffocated made her scream all the more. When John finally realised she was dreaming, most of the hotel was awake and the manager knocking on the door. Poor John was dubious whether his explanations were quite accepted, and the following day Joan overheard two women talking about her as the poor little bride whose brute of a husband beat her up in the night. They certainly took some getting used to, those nightmares, and we were not at all surprised that John had forgotten all our warnings at his first experience of one. Of course he had heard her before when he had stayed at Labis, but it's quite a different matter being in the same room, as well I knew.

JOAN AND JOHN kept their promise to me about staying with them, so when Mummy and Charles returned from one of the visits to Singapore of Johore Bahru, they left me behind. I loved being with them, although there was one thing that marred my visits, and this was John's addiction to the whisky bottle. This had been some concern to Mummy and Charles before they were married, although I was oblivious of it, and they hoped that after they had settled down he would keep his consumption to a reasonable level. Sometimes I heard Joan protest, 'Not *another* one,' which he would laugh off with a kiss, so I never took much notice until one night I woke to hear them having a row and Joan in tears.

The bedrooms were very close and open so it was practically impossible to ignore it. I got out of bed and went to their room and told John he was cruel to make Joan cry, but I was not prepared for him furiously ordering me back to bed and telling me not to interfere in things I knew nothing about. I was so upset, as he had never been cross with me before, that of course I started to weep too. Joan soothed me down, and came back to me to my room until we were both calmer. She begged me not to tell Mummy, and then next day everything was back to normal and no reference was made to the night before.

I really was very fond of John, and could not relate him to the rather frightening person I had glimpsed. Joan told me she was sure all would be well, but she did not mention until years later, that at that time she had tried to teach him a lesson by getting drunk herself. *She* did not drink at all so it must have been quite an effort to make herself consume large quantities of red wine. This was at dinner one night in their own house, but apparently the only effect it had on John was to make him laugh, and Joan ended in being violently sick.

When they went out in the evening I had to go too. It was not considered 'safe' to leave a girl of my age alone in the house with Chinese servants. Naturally I was only too delighted, especially as most of their friends were young bachelors, and we had some hilarious wild evenings with them. There were four of them who lived in a mess out at Katong, four miles from the town. Their bungalow was situated with one or two others beside a lake, which was surrounded with casuarina trees. My favourite was Trevor Watkins, who was not only handsome, but also seemed to live a dangerous and exciting life rounding up the local pirates in fast motor boats belonging to the Government Customs and Excise Department, which he worked for.

They were all completely uninhibited and thought nothing of ending the evening with most of the furniture wrecked. Admittedly it was all old and rickety and often a chair would collapse under someone's weight, and amidst roars of laughter this would be the signal to throw something around. The old cook and boy took it all in their stride, and presumably set to work the next day and mended it. The cook was quite an artist and produced beautifully modelled mashed potato in the shape of a cow or horse, which it seemed a shame to spoil by digging into, but his favourite pudding was straightforward chocolate blancmange which none of us liked. Directly we all had large helpings on our plates and the boy had left the room, someone would throw it up to the ceiling where it would land with a large splosh. We then all followed suit until the ceiling was dripping and stained with a various assortment of patterns. I thought it marvellous fun, as nobody worried about the mess.

There was a diving board at the end of the garden into the lake, and the evening seldom ended without someone being pushed into the water. I secretly hoped it would happen to me one night, but was slightly taken aback, and Joan more so, when I was actually thrown in one moonlit night. I was almost immediately hauled out, and went home in a variety of borrowed men's clothing with my hair clinging to my head.

It was the same time 'the fleet' came in and I lost my heart completely for the first time. His name was Majendie so of course everyone called him Madge. He and his friend known as 'Sharkie' Armstrong would turn up at the house and want to take us all out. Sharkie had a big round red face and looked like Jack Oakie, a film star of that time, always playing the fool and making everyone laugh, but Madge was quieter and so thoughtful, and I thought him perfection. They took us over their submarine and promised one day to take us out to sea, but sadly this never happened. Neither did Madge come back to Labis as planned for the weekend when I had to return. I was in seventh heaven at the thought, and so it seemed as if the bottom had fallen out of my world, when Joan told me it all had to be cancelled. Apparently Madge was ill and we could not even go on board to see him as he was in a lot of pain. I thought he must be dying, and nobody explained that it was only a bad go of 'piles', which for some reason seemed to be an unmentionable subject. In the end I had to return to Labis with only a letter to console me. I slept with it under my pillow for some time, but I never saw him again as the fleet had sailed by the time I returned.

Joan and I often spent our mornings going round the native shops where every type of material, Indian saris, and Chinese and Japanese coats, could be bought for a ridiculously low price. There was one Japanese shop called 'Itchey goya' where the silks and cottons were all beautifully laid out in glass-fronted shelves like books, row upon row of segregated colours. You sat on raised platforms covered with matting, while a smiling and very polite assistant spread the gorgeous materials around you. Having viewed what seemed the whole stock, and then bought one yard of material, you were still treated like a queen and bowed out with no apparent ill-will. In fact, just the opposite; you were begged to come again. Charles insisted that this was only good trade and surface politeness, and that in reality they disliked all Europeans. We found this hard to believe, as wherever we went, whether it was among the Japanese or Chinese, Indians or Malays, we were met with the same smiling faces who soon recognised us, and they would call out to us to come in and look around.

All the shops were open-fronted, and there would be whole streets selling the same merchandise. In an Arab street, you could buy all types of native sandals, and the Malay national garments, including the men's velvet hats shaped almost like a glengarry. The sarongs in bright cottons made up into attractive morning dresses, and the lovely silk ones, many hand embroidered in gold and silver thread, could be used for the evening. But at this time few European women seemed to realise the marvellous potential at their doorstep and preferred to use imported materials.

Sometimes we spent the whole day at the swimming club. There was no pool and we bathed in the sea in a *pagar* which was an enclosure made out of bamboo stakes and designed to keep out the sharks. One felt quite safe inside, but there was a gruesome story of a girl who had her leg bitten off by a shark that had got inside the *pagar* during an exceptionally high tide. Some brave man had dived in and got her back on to the diving board, but she had died from loss of blood. After this the sides were heightened.

We revelled in the clear warm water, staying in most of the morning. It was easy enough to forget the strength of the sun, and by sitting in the sea on the edge of the sand, one could get badly sunburned, even with a good protecting tan. We soon learned never to do this unless we continuously poured oil over our shoulders. Contrary to many popular beliefs that it fried, we found that far the best thing to use was olive oil. We would have our lunch in the club house and then still in our bathing dresses – which dried on us in a few minutes – stretch ourselves on long basket chairs on the verandah and sleep or read. John would often join us for lunch and then return to his office and come back again with several friends to bathe and have tea. By 5.00 p.m. it would be cooler and it was a relief to take off their office suits – even though these were made of white duck, but with tight high necks – and plunge into the sea. We would stay on until it was dark and the lights from the city were reflected across the bay, only a few miles away.

During the weekends we either sailed from the yacht club or best of all, rented a little bungalow at Changi, a village about fifteen miles from Singapore, situated on the coast a short way up the Johore Straits but within sight of the open sea. There was no road to the few rather primitive thatched houses built on a long stretch of sand fringed with coconut trees. We left the car at the mouth of the Changi River and walking over a footbridge and then about half a mile on to the beach. We had to take all our supplies for the weekend, including water, but there would be plenty of small boys willing to carry these for a few cents. The sand was almost white and the sea, warm and very blue and clear. There was a Chinese caretaker and his wife who cooked and looked after the house. There was a *koleh* (Malay boat) with the house to use for sailing and fishing. It was fascinating how easy it was to catch a great variety of beautiful fish by merely dropping a baited line over the side. Most of them were good to eat, but there was one the Malays disliked intensely as it had very sharp rabbit-like teeth that would bite through the line. If one was brought into the boat, it would blow itself up into a round ball, at the same time letting out little squeaks.

Sometimes I walked along the sands to a place called Teluh Paku, which was round the corner and faced the open sea. The houses here were all stone built and used and owned for holidays

Joan [author's sister] with John and the author at Changi

by various European firms. I had told Charles on my return to Labis how nice these looked and one of them belonged to the agents of the estate, so he was able to rent it and we all went for a holiday there with Joan and John joining us at weekends. There always seemed to be a breeze except at low tide, and then there were miles of sand and pools filled with a variety of fish and crabs and even the exotic little seahorses.

There were a few young children staying at the other houses whom I would take for walks – without their amahs – and we had fun discovering all this life in the pools and collecting them in tin buckets. It seemed as if John was better, or if he was drinking too much, not in front of the family, and Joan was far too loyal to split on him. In fact they seemed very happy, although I know Joan wished she could have a baby.

When we returned to Labis after this holiday, it was to be for the last time before we had to pack up and return to England. I dreaded it, particularly the parting from Mummy. The plan was for her to stay on in England when Charles returned to Malaya in six months time. She would see me settled in a boarding school, and then go back and join him. I would spend my holidays with the Gabriel cousins who lived quite near the school. I knew I would eventually return to Malaya, but the four years at school stretched ahead like eternity. It was unlikely that my beloved Pups would still be alive, and a good home had to be found for the pony. We dispatched her in a cattle truck from the station to a family who lived on an estate near Kuala Lumpur. My heart nearly broke hearing her neigh as we left her and went back to the house.

It seemed as if the world was coming to an end, and of course this particular one was. It would never be quite the same again. Even the cookie and boys wept when we finally departed and it was agony hugging the dogs for the hundredth last time. When we got to the station everyone was there to wave us goodbye, and Mummy and I cried most of the way down to Singapore. We stayed a few days with Joan and John, and then had another tearful farewell. This at least was eased by the knowledge that they were to come home on leave themselves within a few months.

It took three weeks to get to Marseilles. As I was just thirteen I had a 'full' fare, which meant I had the best of both worlds, and made the most of it. I was allowed to do more or less as I wanted, as long as I reported to Mummy and Charles every now and them. Sometimes I ate with them, but more often than not had my dinner with the ship's officers who, with the exception of the captain and first officer, ate before the passengers and they invited me to join them. Mummy and Charles did not object to this, as they thought they were a nice lot, and I would come to no harm. I developed a passion for Tony Cox, the third officer. He was big and jolly with a round pink face, and he would let me walk round the deck with him when he did his 'after dinner' patrol while most of the passengers were still eating.

There was a girl of my age whom I made friends with. She came from Shanghai and had some pretty hair-raising tales to tell. Despite her apparent sophistication, I suspected quite a lot of them were made up to impress what she took to be a simple girl straight from the Malayan jungle.

We went ashore at all the ports. The first was Colombo where again we visited Mount Lavinia, but we also had time the following day to motor up into the hills to Kandy, a lovely drive through the tea plantations. The next place was Aden. Here there had been no rain for *seven* years and the huge water tanks were completely empty. The local small boys used them as a trap for the tourists, swarming down the sides and calling up from the dry bottom, with their voices echoing up in a most impressive way, for us to throw them down a few cents. Apparently soon after this the rains came, and so I suppose the boys lost their source of revenue.

Port Said still held its magic. One or two of the older and more reputable Arab men who did conjuring tricks were allowed on board to the delight of not only the younger passengers. Their main trick was to produce day old chickens from every conceivable place. This was wholly fascinating as we were all clustered round them on the deck with no question of any pre-arranged stage management. After producing several baby chickens from behind my ear, one of them asked me to put a *2s. 6d.* bit in my palm, holding it tight and closing my hand. If it turned out to be a penny could he keep it? Of course I agreed, so he murmured several MAGIC words over me and then asked me, very politely, 'Please Missie you now open,' and although I had held tight to my original coin, sure enough it was now turned into a penny which he quickly removed from me. This really did seem like magic, or was it an optical illusion?

Ashore one was pursued by swarms of Egyptians trying to sell something, or doing tricks while one sat outside a café, or charming a snake, but all with a gift of the gab which eventually disarmed the most hardened traveller like Charles, even if only 'to get rid of the blighters'.

Only too soon we were in the Mediterranean and heading for Marseilles where we were to leave the ship and take a train across France. More farewells, and once again we left the separate world of life on board a ship, and were plunged into the reality of facing our friends and relations after a three year separation.

It was wonderful to see Jack, who had grown into a young man, but was still the same to me. He and some of my girl friends were on the station to meet us, and Clara was soon round to the hotel weeping tears of joy to see us again. My friends wasted no time in telling me I could not possibly wear those ghastly brown stockings. These had been sent for by Mummy as part of my 'warm trousseau' little knowing that they had gone out of fashion. So out we went to buy the pale fawn ones which Iris and Yvonne assured me were then the correct wear.

Apart from my stockings, I felt very strange and out of things and kept wondering how long it would take me to settle down and conform. I never did completely, although I enjoyed being with my cousins again, and regaled them with stories, no doubt often exaggerated, of my doings in Malaya, which made up for any superiority they felt as young men of fifteen and sixteen towards a girl of thirteen.

The school I went to was only a few miles away from where they lived. I started as a day girl, as Mummy thought this would be easier for me. I made friends, and by my second term, I had begun to adjust myself to the new life, but was shattered when the time came for Mummy to leave. The school made a special concession and allowed me to go home to my cousins every weekend, so although the younger boys were at boarding school, I had Jack who came down from London where he was working in my Uncle's office. He and I spent hours discussing how we would go to Malaya together once I had finished with school.

He did not really enjoy working in London, and planned to find a job in Malaya.

I was always being accused of 'day dreaming' in class, and certainly spent a lot of time thinking of all that had happened in the three years I had been away. My mother wrote me long letters keeping me in touch with all that went on, including the excitement when Charles officially declared the new road open, which put Labis 'on the map'. I could not wait to get back and see it all for myself.

The time eventually came, but it seemed a very long four years.

Part Two
Return to Malaya
(1930–1941)

MUMMY AND CHARLES had come home on leave in 1930, and I left school for good that summer. They took a furnished house in Instow, North Devon, and we spent the rest of the summer there. It was a wonderful place for young people, and there were plenty of them of my age. We sailed, bathed and picnicked mostly in big groups, danced at the local hotel and in private houses, and generally had what we called 'a marvellous time' with more young men than girls for a change. Dick Beckwith was one of the young men, just commissioned in the Navy and who we continued to see off and on for the next ten years. Joan and John, also on leave, came down to stay. I met them at the station, and I had grown so much they did not at first recognise me. I rather fancied myself in a get-up of white pleated skirt and royal blue cardigan and beret copied from some 'older woman' who I admired.

In late September we went back to a flat in London for the three weeks before we set sail for Malaya. My dream had come true at last. We had a perfect four weeks on board the P&O liner *Mantua*, stopping at all the places twice visited before, but not as a grown-up. Again there were more young men on board then girls, so we were escorted ashore with a percentage of one female to four males. We danced every night on deck by the light of the moon (how much more romantic than the present day air-conditioned saloon), and finally arrived in Malaya. First to Penang – lovely bathing on this perfect island, and night life at the Runneymeade Hotel. We lived in a whirl and never came down to earth, even in Singapore where we were met and taken round the town. Ella and Jack Frewen, friends of Joan's, suggested that I stayed on with them for a couple of weeks, while my mother and Charles went on ahead to the Estate. The offer was very tempting as I liked Ella tremendously; she was tall and pretty, with beautiful auburn hair, and was great fun to be with. She was older then I was, but younger than Joan. We had a very gay time with masses of parties, swimming at Tanglin or the Singapore swimming clubs, and every weekend out at Changi, on a long strip of palm-lined beach with a few privately owned simple bungalows. The bathing there was perfect, and it almost broke my heart when later the army took over the whole strip, cutting down all the coconut trees and ruining the place. As it was on the entrance to the naval base and open China Sea, it was obviously considered necessary.

Singapore was still reeling from the impact of Noel Coward, who had just spent a month there. The friend he was travelling with was taken ill with amoebic dysentery. During the enforced stay, he looked around for something to do. Evidently life in the town was NOT his idea of fun. He found a group of English actors, members of a troupe of strolling players called 'The Quaints', whose strolls took them all over the Far East in the late twenties and early thirties. They were then playing at the Victoria Theatre in Singapore, with a company that included Betty Hare and a twenty-two year-old John Mills. Their repertoire included R. C. Sheriff's war play *Journey's End.* They persuaded Noel to take over the part of Stanhope (having temporarily lost one of their leading men). Coward, having nothing better to do while his friend was in hospital, agreed to play for three performances. To the audience (which included the governor Sir Cecil and Lady Clemetie), who seldom had the opportunity to see an actor of Coward's distinction in their corner of the world, Coward's intense, undisciplined, neurotic performance as Captain Stanhope, was received with respect by all except the critic of the *Straits Times*, who found the nerve to point out that Noel was unlikely casting for the gallant tight-lipped officer, and that his portrayal of Stanhope as 'a whimpering neurotic prig' was NOT what the author or *he* had in mind. Apparently Coward had the decency to admit he agreed with the criticism, but had blotted his copy-book further by writing, after spending a few days as guest of the Clementies at Government House, a witty, though cruel, ditty, about his hostess, which upset the older generation who considered it in very bad taste. I cannot remember it all, but some of it went roughly like this:

Whoops, Lady Clementie,
You must have been inhibited at twenty,
Rather dull at thirty-four,
At forty-four a bore,
You really are the fountain-head
Of fun in Singapore.

Whoops, Lady Clementie,
You must have read a lot of G. H. Henty,
You've not read Bertram Russell,
And you've not read Dr Freud
So maybe that's the reason
Why you look so unenjoyed.

I must say I thought it very amusing, although I did not agree with his verdict, though I could see what he meant when I later attended a Garden Party and Ball at Government House.

At last – back at Labis things looked just the same, and the only real change was that the road was through, and Mummy and Charles thought nothing of motoring into Segamat, fifteen miles north in in the evening, to play golf and tennis at the Club. This opened up a new life, and again there were so many young men starved of female company.

I had no horse to ride because of the 'slump'. Pups was still alive but quite a staid old dog, though he seemed to remember me. I decided to use what funds I had in visiting Joan and John in Singapore. They were back from their leave, and told me to go down to them whenever I got bored with life on the Estate. The young men around were not all that exciting, so I found myself going for a week or so each month. Life in Singapore was fun, but after a time both Joan and I started to get bored with the main female amusement of playing majong or bridge each morning. We had been left a small legacy and with this decided to start a dress shop. The local Chinese tailors were excellent but needed guidance, so we thought there was quite a need for a shop where women could come and order a dress, and discuss it with a European woman. (Joan was good at designing.) We had an instant success when we set up in Raffles Square and were inundated with orders. We suggested we made this or that in native material, which we considered was not used nearly enough, most women thinking everything they wore had to come from Europe. We often managed to persuade them otherwise, and as chief 'buyer', I had a lot of fun taking John's car down to the native quarters of Arab Streets, Northbridge Road, etc, which I knew so well, and collecting marvellous patterns for some particular order. I got to know all the shopkeepers, and they gave me what amounted to trade prices, particularly as I could speak to them in Malay. Prices were fantastically low – pure silk at two shillings and sixpence a yard. About this time I had quite an amusing incident which, if I had followed it up, could have changed my whole life.

I was asked to a lunch party at Raffles Hotel to meet an American comedy team called 'Wheeler and Wolsey', who were doing a world tour to promote their latest film. They had a great following in most countries, as the brand of humour was such that you could understand without knowing the language. They were very much in the style of the present-day couple 'Morecambe and Wise', and quite similar in looks too. I sat next to Wolsey, who was the smaller and more dapper of the two. He consumed several drinks to my one, and got very expansive, telling me that I looked just like Joan Bennet, and that if I went to Hollywood he would make me into a great star. He got so insistent, even to suggest I rang up my parents and got permission to go with them when they left for Hong Kong the next day. At eighteen I was, perhaps, secretly rather impressed, but not so naive as to not realise the implications of what would be expected in return. So I kept my head sufficiently to smile at him sweetly, and say that, although I felt very flattered, I did not think it was a thing one could make up one's mind about in a few minutes. After lunch he insisted upon seeing me home in a huge hired American open tourer (where we both sat at the back on either side,) in order, I suppose, partly to cool his head and, possibly, to try and persuade me further to accept his offer, but he soon fell silent when he realised I was adamant in my refusal; and whether in disgust at my lack of co-operation, or because he just could not contain himself, he gave an enormous belch and spat right across my front and into the road. I was slightly taken back, although admiring the aim, but it quite settled any lingering thoughts I might have had about trying my luck in Hollywood. Naturally that was the last I ever heard of him, despite his goodbyes and promises to 'follow up'.

This way of life went on for a year or two until Joan's marriage with John was beginning to break up. He was sadly still drinking pretty heavily, and with no children to pull things together they were drifting further and further apart. Joan had many admirers, and by this time I had met and got engaged to Roper. I went back to Labis quite often and he would come up for weekends, driving me either up to the Estate or back to Singapore. Luckily everyone approved of Roper, though he was known in Singapore as rather a recluse, spending his weekends shooting and fishing with his Malays, rather than joining in with the social night life. All the same he had one 'weakness', and this was horse racing. This was where we met, and afterwards on the same evening at a party given by him and two friends – three of them lived together in an old bungalow. I had been invited to go to this party with Joan and John, but had to refuse as I already had a 'date'. This ended about 2.00 a.m. and when fast asleep I was woken by Joan telephoning from the swimming club where at 4.00 a.m. they were still at it. She said I must join them, and she was sending some man back to pick me up. It was Roper and we never looked back from that date, and were engaged before the end of the next week.

For various reasons, mostly financial (his family business of Boustead & Co. – started by his Grandfather – insisted upon their assistants earning so much before they were allowed to get married) we had to wait eight months before getting married. Even then we cheated over this, by saying I had £1,000 a year of my own, when in actual fact it was more like £5,000 in capital. All the same we felt this would see us through, and after winding up the shop, had a little more to add. Anyway, the Uncles, and the Chairman in Singapore – Oscar Maas – were persuaded that we had enough to satisfy the very rigid rules made by the firm,

Roper, 1934

and we set a date for 10 March, 1934. Joan was going back to England soon afterwards, with Mummy and Charles, who were due for leave. Joan was getting a divorce, and despite various men wanting to marry her once she was free, she had made no promises.

Our wedding took place in the Cathedral, with Joan as Matron of Honour and Alec Fairlie as Best Man. The reception was held at Abbotsford, the beautiful old house where the Chairman of Bousteads always lived. We spent one night at Seaview Hotel, and the next day drove up to Port Dickson, a small place on the west coast, where years before Charles had taken us for a holiday from Labis. We had a bungalow right on the beach and forgot ourselves enough to get badly sunburnt during the next two days. At least I did and suffered some agony for a day or two. We then motored up to Frasers Hill for a week and on to the Cameron Highlands for two days as Roper had never been to any of these places, having been stuck in Singapore, and taking his one and only local leave in Borneo. We got up very early in order to get to Kuala Lumpur in time for a day's racing, and then down to Singapore and out to our 'island retreat' for the rest of the time.

The island was about thirty-six acres and in the Straits of Johore between Changi and the naval base, and was called Pulau Serangoon. It had a very attractive Malay attap-roofed house built out over the sea on stilts, and our old Malay boatman, Sarleh, whom Roper had been going fishing and shooting with for years, had told us about it. It was deserted except for one old Chinese fisherman who lived in a tiny hut on the other side of the island. Sarleh had found out that we could rent the whole place from a Chinese for £10 a year. Cheap though it was, we had not got £10 to spare, (so when we had met a friend at Raffles Hotel one night, he asked us what we wanted for a wedding present, we said 'an island').

We had gone out during weekends and bought enough furniture for it to start us off, but this was the first time we had slept there. Sarleh took us over in his old boat which was always having engine trouble, and left us with a tiny Koleh-Malayan very light canoe, but came back now and then with stores and to take us out fishing. It was heaven. The water was very clear, and at high

Island House off Singapore Island (up the straights from the Naval base) used for weekend fishing

tide it came right up to the top of the wooden jetty which stuck out from the sitting-room. Our bedroom floor was practically awash too. There was a tiny sandy beach along either side of the house and a few palms; the rest was mangroves and scrub inland. When the tide was out parts were muddy, but one could walk quite a long way without sinking and find all sorts of fascinating creatures left in the pools, including minute seahorses.

At last we had to go back to Singapore and work, but planned to spend most of our weekends there. We had rented a small new house five miles out on the Bukit Timah road near the racecourse. It was set back about five hundred yards from the main road, up a country lane, and ending in a nicely planted garden with scrub land behind. We had a huge dog called Oscar. He had belonged to someone in the Boustead mess, who had got him from a Captain of one of the glen boats that plied up the coast as far as Vladivostok. Here the Captain's Danish bulldog had met a 'Camchatka' hound (whatever that might be), and Oscar was one of the results. He was about the size of a tall labrador, white rough coat with fawn markings and a marvellous temperament. He adopted us, and apart from a few nights out on the tiles, he never left us. On the island were a few pathetic stray bitches – local pidogs. Nobody knew how they got there, and the old Chinese said he was not responsible. We fed them as they were near to starving, living on raw fish and any scraps they could find. Oscar, of course, dealt with them all in turn, and gradually they all disappeared as word had got round; the local Chinese liked to get their hands on a 'good dog', and Oscar was much admired by them.

Mummy, Charles and Joan had left for home soon after our marriage, so although we both had friends in Singapore, we spent nearly all our spare time gardening and going for walks with Oscar – there was quite a lot of country up above the house – and during the racing season, would get up early (5.00 a.m.) and go up to the racecourse and watch the gallops. Roper studied 'form', and in the first eighteen months of our marriage we made eighty pounds. It was quite a large sum in those day.

I had a miscarriage, and as I had had malaria quite badly for eight months or so, by the time we were finally due for leave after five years in Malaya, we were both badly in need of a change

Author with Oscar

of climate. We took Oscar back to live at the Boustead Mess where the head boy had known him since a puppy and could be relied on to feed him. All the same, we heard from some Malays who lived up our road, that he went the five and a half miles back to our house every day to look for us for the six months we were away.

We went home by boat which was a nice rest-cure as it took four weeks, and arrived in England about October. We went straight to Roper's parents whom I had never met, and they were both such sweet exceptional people, who I loved immediately. We had decided to spend our leave in Norfolk, and from a friend of Roper's parents we rented a farmhouse for four months and a small shoot nearby. We had a wonderful time there, and Roper bought me a gun and taught me to shoot. There was a beautiful hundred-acre wood with the shoot, and we spent a lot of time there, shooting rabbits and the odd pheasant and duck.

The time went only too quickly and before we knew it we were back in Singapore. After a year we had a son and called him Mark. We both had a horror of Chinese amahs, so engaged a Eurasian girl called Rosie. She was 'mission' educated and spoke quite good English and did as I asked her, so all went well and the Chinese cook and his wife did not seem to resent her.

When Mark was about three months, we changed house and went to live on the coast near Katong, and near Rosie's home. It was quite a startling house by the average Singapore standards,and had been built by a rich Chinese gentleman for his concubines. He had visited Hollywood and come back and described the houses he had seen there to a Eurasian architect. His main house where he lived with number one wife was some way below the one for the concubines, which was up quite a steep incline. The story went that after a week of climbing up the hill for a bit of extra sex he had a heart attack and died. Anyway, we saw a 'to let' notice and were so enchanted with what we found that we decided to take it, although it was eight miles to the office. We never regretted it, and it was the nicest and coolest house we had ever known. All the rooms were large, with downstairs green tiled floors and a staircase which led to the main sitting-room and three bedrooms. The sitting-room was in the centre with three French windows overlooking the magnificent view over the China Sea and the Dutch Islands. The road below was out of sight, as there was a grass tennis court and trees hiding it, and at the back scrub land and hills. The bedroom all stuck out from the central room so had three outside walls with windows to each, to catch any breeze. We never used mosquito nets, and sometimes even slept on the flat roof which had a pagoda with bougainvillaea growing up it. There was a 'watch-tower' higher up, where the view was even better and which seemed quite up in the air. There were some Australians living in the old man's 'number one' house below, but we thought it did not compare with ours.

We had two wonderful years there. *Sarleh*, the Malay boatman, asked if he could bring his family (and boat) and work for us, he as gardener and two of his daughters, Norsiah and Pendy, in the house. There was a lot of room at the back by the garages, quite apart from the Chinese quarters, so we agreed to let them come. There were seven of them, as two of their children were married.

Everyone who came to the house remarked on Mark's suntan and pink cheeks, as the average European child tended to look a bit white and peaky. People seemed frightened of taking them out in the sun, but if one was careful about a hat and oiling their skins, it did not seem to do any harm, and in his case the reverse. He was 'put out' on the roof-garden on a camp bed from 7.00 a.m. to 8.00 a.m. and then after breakfast would sleep in a pram on the verandah until twelve, then again from two to four in his cool airy bedroom, then out in the garden for another hour in his pram, and after this he either played in the tennis court (an ideal play-pen) or Rosie or we would take him down to the beach across the road. He had this routine for two years and seemed to thrive on it, ate and slept marvellously, but was very active in between.

I often went and rode in the early morning. Some Australians had a sheep farm not far along the coast and they also kept quite a lot of horses, mostly ex-racers. One could ride along the sandy beach or among the coconut plantations which had a lot of dirt tracks. I usually took Oscar with me, and one day I had an exceptionally nervous horse who had only just arrived. I had to get him past a Chinese lorry which back-fired, and he immediately took off towards the main Changi road. I realised I was not going to be able to stop him, and had visions of colliding with a car. Just as I was thinking I should throw myself off, the stirrup leather broke and I found myself in the ditch. As I got up I saw both horse and Oscar disappearing in a cloud of dust towards the road. I started to run, and by the time I got to the end a Chinese had stopped them both, and the horse was grazing calmly by the wayside. There were a few Chinese shop-houses and everyone was out to have a 'look', talking at the top of their voices. I managed to collect both horse and Oscar, and was standing trying to get the sand out of my hair when a convoy of army trucks went by on the main road with a crowd of interested and shouting jocks leaning out, and a few officers trying to keep straight faces. Afterwards I discovered these were Gordon Highlanders and among them were 'Dukie' and Michael Harter, soon to become two of our greatest friends. They told me they were fairly surprised at the scene I presented, and felt they should have stopped and helped, but were already late for their assignment and anyway obviously I was all in one piece. I was too, just, and managed to mount and *walk* the horse back to the farm.

Soon after this we met a lot of the Gordons at a party at Changi and I had my leg pulled once they realised I was the girl with the dog and the horse. They could see nothing of my face apparently but a mass of blonde hair. Dukie and Michael started to come to our house regularly and, as they liked doing the same things as us, often came out to the island, and on our fishing and shooting expeditions. Soon after this a girl friend of mine came out to stay. I had known Yvonne ever since we went to kindergarten together in London. We had various parties to introduce her to people, but it soon became evident that she and Dukie had fallen for each other. They got engaged, and when Yvonne went home Dukie followed her on his leave. They were married just before we got home for OUR leave in 1939.

By this time we had achieved another boy, Rory, and he was only six weeks when we set sail in a Dutch ship, the *Dempo*, accompanied by a marvellous Irish woman called Mrs Flynn. I had advertised for someone to help us with the two children in the voyage, and she had replied. She was the answer to anyone's prayer. Little, dark, bright and cheerful, and *so* efficient and sweet. Mr Flynn was in some firm who did not pay their wives' passages home on leave, hence the answer to our advertisement. But apart from this, she was willing to come six weeks in advance when I went into hospital to have Rory, and even a week before that, so Mark could get used to her. Rosie stayed on until we left, but wouldn't take the responsibility on her own.

Poor Rory got a chill in his pram on deck and the Dutch doctor insisted he spent the rest of the voyage in the cabin. This complicated matters somewhat, but Mrs Flynn was so marvellous and we managed between us. We had Mark in our cabin (there was a communicating door) at night, as Rory often yelled and woke Mark up. This was all right except that at about 6.00 a.m. he wanted the 'pottie', and this got steadily earlier and earlier as we put the clock back twenty minutes or so a day. In the end he was wanting to pee at 3.00 a.m. and then would often not go back to sleep. In desperation Roper would take him up on deck about 6.00 a.m., armed with his miniature camp bed, strap him into it, and they both sat apart, drinking orange juice and reading for an hour or so, until I and Mrs Flynn had surfaced and took over. Mark was quite happy over the arrangement as long as he had plenty of books and could see Roper. At last we arrived in Southampton to be met by Joan with our new car, and were whisked off to Rock Lodge, Roper's mother's house in Sussex.

When we were in Port Said Roper had bought a *Field* (the *Field Magazine*) and seen in it a place advertised in Norfolk called Foulden Hall, to let with shooting. He had kept it, and on the off-chance of it still going, he rang up the agents who said it belonged to Lord Amhurst who had not let it, and sent the particulars which seemed perfect for our requirements. We decided to go up by car (we had had our first new car ever, delivered on arrival, a rather smart Ford V8 coupé). Mrs Flynn was still with us, but I had been trying to get someone to take her place as her husband had got home and naturally wanted his wife to join him, though she seemed in no particular hurry, and had got very fond of the children. Anyway, it gave us time to go up on our own and stay with Roper's friends, the Lloyds, and see the place. It was very attractive, quite a large house, and there was a cook, a Mrs Jessop, who was willing to 'carry on' with us, a parlour maid, Mavis Dunbar, and a tweeny, Eva Stocking, whose wages at fifteen were five shillings a week. The other two received a pound (for the cook) and eighteen shillings (for the maid).

The Dowager Lady Amhurst showed us round and must have got hold of some idea that we came from the Middle East instead of the Far East, as she suggested that our 'Arabs' could pitch their tents in a field beyond the front part of the garden. We assured her that we had no Arabs, but I don't think she took it in. The garden was a paradise for children, and in the walled part there was a bricked stream running through, perfect for toy boats, ending in large, but well fenced ponds. Roper was thrilled with the prospect of the shoot and old Daisley's – the keeper's – graphic description of the game likely to be had. There was a lot of water on the place so good duck shooting too. He was a dear old man who seemed to love having anyone as keen and knowledgeable as Roper to go out with. The shoot consisted of 1,374 acres, and the rent for some eight months – June to February – was £250 including the house. We took it, and moved up there in the first week of June.

By this time I had engaged Betty Webber as a Nanny. She was just the right kind of person for us, and the children, who took to her at once. Betty was married to a gunner, Peter Webber, who at the time of Munich had given up a very successful florist business, and in a moment of patriotism, had joined up and when told he was to be sent to Singapore, asked Betty, who had helped his mother look after a step-sister and brother, to marry him. This she had done, and had answered my advertisement for someone willing to go out to Singapore with us the following February. She assured me that once we got there, there was no chance of her being able to live with Peter, and all they hoped for was to meet once a week or so, and for him to be able to come to our house to visit her. As Roper's position once we returned was to be Acting Chairman, it meant we would have to entertain quite a bit, and it was essential therefore to have someone who we could happily leave the children with. So Mrs Flynn, with many tears, left us, and Betty took over. She was with us, on and off, for over twelve years and became one of our dearest friends, and I do not remember ever having a cross word.

The time at Foulden passed only too quickly. All the family

visited us at different times, and Joan brought one of her boy-friends down (who she later married), and proceeded to have one of her famous nightmares, screaming that the Germans were coming and there was an air-raid taking place. Quite unnerving, as we were all only too conscious of the fact that we were sitting on a volcano that would erupt at any moment. When it did happen, in September, apart from making an air-raid shelter in the cellar, and getting a bit tight on VERY old bottles of champagne (these had been laid down years ago and were well past their prime, so we felt entitled to sample them) we carried on as before, far removed from all signs of war.

Finally the time to go back to Singapore arrived. We went up to London in early February 1940 with the idea of flying to Paris, and from there getting a train to Genoa where we would join a Dutch ship (Holland was still out of the war), and hope to get to Singapore without mishap or black-out. The first thing that happened was a complete 'freeze' and non 'take-off' from London. We played it to the last possible moment, and even went with Dick Beckwith (later of *The Prince of Wales*, the Royal Navy battleship sunk by the Japanese in 1942) and others to see 'Bye Bye Blackbird'.

The next day as the freeze was still on, we trained down to Folkestone, and dripping 'cream of wheat' and wet napkins all the way from the station to the Folkestone Hotel, we booked in and tried to sleep or rest. The French boat train did not get in until 10.00 p.m., and we were not booked with sleepers, we had been told that the first on board would – with a little financial persuading – get a berth. This we did, and the purser offered us his own accommodation for ten shillings. He demonstrated that by putting two life-jackets on the floor we could all sleep there, and comfortably. As there were only two bunks and a sofa, we left it all to Betty, and went in search of something else for ourselves. I found the Ladies very grand and large and deserted, so quickly staked my claim by putting some belongings on to one of the red plush divans which surrounded the room.

Directly the train came in the place was swarming with people. Roper unfortunately had come out of the Gents cloakroom, which anyway was far smaller than the Ladies, to see if Betty and I were all right, so by the time he got back, every place had been taken and he spent the rest of the night on the floor. I got up about 7.00 a.m. and went on deck to find not only thick fog, but Roper almost unrecognisable as he had forgotten to undo his collar, and so because of this and the draught on the floor, his face had swollen. We asked one of the sailors about any hope we had of setting sail by 8.00 a.m. to which his only reply was a shrug. If we were late we would miss our connection in Paris, so it was like a miracle when, after some breakfast, the fog suddenly lifted and we were off.

The Channel was mined and we went horribly close to a floating one, but arrived safely, and then had rather a nightmare train journey to Paris. We got a carriage to ourselves and had plenty of food in a hamper for the children and Betty, but we had to queue up for hours in the corridor for lunch, though it was excellent when we finally got it about 3.00 p.m. We had a metre stove to cook Rory's cereal on, but it was so slow, and I shall never forget his screams of hunger, with Betty and I feverishly trying to get it to come to the boil in near darkness (as the trains were blacked out), and thinking it would never be cooked before we arrived in Paris. However, we just made it, and then had a dash across Paris to another station where we were met by a 'Cook's Courier' and shown to two sleeping compartments.

We left Betty to get the children to bed and, on the advice of the Cook's man, went in search of a hamper of food, as there was none on the train, and we would not arrive in Genoa until 11.00 a.m. the next day. When we got back, armed with an excellent hamper, we found some woman claiming our sleeper. She had been issued with the same number as ours. Finally, after a great deal of argument, we persuaded the French wagon-lit attendant to give *us* an empty First Class apartment, which only had one bunk. Mrs Smith, the woman in question, had a friend with her, so we left her in the original sleeper and decided to make the best of our one First Class bunk.

Betty and the children were asleep by this time, so we tucked into cold chicken, crisp rolls and butter, and a bottle of wine and cheese. War, or no war, the French knew how to provide. The attendant came back for a chat (money had passed between us to even achieve our one bunk), and after a glass of wine he managed to convey that by making us 'Second Class', he could turn our sleeper into a double one merely by pulling down a second berth. So after all, we both managed to sleep. We had been warned on leaving Paris to lock our doors, as we stopped at a border town where a lot of French troops were stationed, and they had once or twice made a lot of trouble by boarding the wagon-lit trains and robbing the passengers. However, we were so exhausted that we heard nothing until the next morning when we woke at a station on the Italian frontier and where, on looking out of the window, we were greeted by the wonderful sight of sunshine, and the Italian police in the fancy-dress of Napoleon hats and white breeches.

The children and Betty had slept well too, and soon we were delighted to find ourselves in two spacious cabins on board the Dutch ship *Dempo.* They had beds instead of bunks, and polished teak floors with rugs. Great luxury, and the whole ship was beautifully equipped with large nurseries and deck space for the children with every conceivable gadget to keep them happy. We all settled down to three weeks of ease and comfort, and found several congenial people.

We went straight out to Katong on our arrival as the house had been rented to a friend – Aubrey Wallich – while we had been away, and both the Chinese and Malays were all there as he had taken them on with the house. Betty's husband, Peter, soon found us and they went off together for the day. We had both the Malay girls, Norsiah and Pendy, helping in the house, and the youngest, Tabah, who was about five (two years older than Mark), enjoyed coming to play with him when he was out in the garden. They all loved and spoiled the children, but were so unobtrusive and would just disappear when they felt they were not wanted. Sarleh, the father, who had kept the garden for us, and his boat down on the shore, wanted to move all his family (there were nine children, but three away married) with us when we went to Abbotsford for a year. Roper was to take over the Chairmanship of Bousteads so Mr and Mrs Cherry could go off on leave to Canada. There was already a huge staff employed there, but some were leaving, so in the end we took our Chinese boy and all the Sarleh family. There was a large compound (about six acres) and masses of outbuildings for the six gardeners and their families, and apparently still room for a few more. The

Chinese servants had quarters near the house joined by a covered way. A census of the population was taken while we were there and there were seventy-five people living on the premises. Lots of these were 'hangers-on' in the shape of grandmothers and other relations, but one would never have guessed there could possibly be that number.

We hated leaving the sea and our house there, but Abbotsford was a beautiful, old and very spacious house, with lovely grounds for the children with masses of tambussa trees. We had bought a canvas pool, and put this up near the side of the house and made a sand pit. They had a nursery, and a bedroom and bathroom, and Betty had a bedroom and private staircase down to a bathroom, with a door out to the garden. This proved to be very useful for the children as well as Peter when he visited Betty, as he could slip in without having to come through the house.

On our side was a bedroom, dressing-room, bath and verandah plus a guest-room and bath downstairs. It was all on such a large scale that it was difficult to realise that there was not more accommodation. The whole length of the front of the house was one large sitting-room, and the verandah continued round the house. We blocked these off so each bedroom had its own private verandah sitting-room. The bathrooms (four) all had white marble floors and walls. Marble floors downstairs which, apart from the two bathrooms, consisted of a huge dining-room, and a billiard-room, leading out onto another verandah where Roper and I breakfasted.

All quite grand living and very comfortable. The only fly in the ointment, as far as I was concerned, was the old Chinese cook who not only had a wall-eye, but was completely set in his ways and menus. He looked upon me as far too young and inexperienced to run an establishment (all the other 'Big Mistress' had been well over forty), so he proceeded to tell me how things should be done. Having often dined there in the past I thought there was room for some improvement, particularly in the choice of menus. He had one set 'dinner party' of which the main course was Quails in Casserole. Every morning after breakfast I had to interview him in the dining-room. Slightly nervous and fixed by the wall-eye, I suggested we changed this and that. I would also like to go to the market myself (which was huge and great fun) and buy the food. As they all made a good 'racket' out of the marketing, this was greeted with pretty sour looks, but I weathered these, and in the end he accepted my freak ideas, though not with very good grace. Still, he was a good cook and the standard of food and variety improved quite a lot. In a way he was not to blame as Mrs Cherry was not interested, and had left the whole of this side to him. She had been Matron of the Singapore hospital before her marriage to Rob Cherry and had still spent a lot of her time doing charity work connected with the medical profession.

Yvonne and Duke were out at Changi, and we saw quite a lot of them as well as other friends, including Dor and Robbie (Robertson). Jack, my brother, was living quite near with his wife Trudy and little girl Jane, who was six months younger than Mark. Altogether we had a happy year there. Roper was preparing to leave for England to do his army training before joining up, and I and the children to go to South Africa, as my mother and Charles were already in the Cape – and it seemed ridiculous to take the children home to Britain. Just before the Cherrys were expected back, it was suggested that Roper could do his training at Changi, where the OCTU operated. This would probably take about nine months, and then he could get a commission in the Gordon Highlanders. Through Dukie and Michael Harter, we had got to know most of the regiment, and the Colonel, Willie Graham, was keen for Roper to join them. This seemed the obvious answer, and meant we could be together all that much longer. Also Betty, who would have stayed with Peter though they had no married quarters, could stay on with us, and if we found a house near Changi, Peter could still continue to visit her whenever he wanted to.

We were lucky and found an old wooden bungalow built on stakes, right on the sea at Tanah Merah. This was only about three miles from Changi, down an earth road alongside Changi gaol. It was perfect for the boys with a few steps down to a sandy beach. All the Sarleh family came with us, and our Chinese boy, Ah-Mo, who had 'a friend' who came as cook. There was a separate stone house which was meant for changing in for bathing, and this we found very useful and used as a summerhouse for meals. There was also a raised platform over the sea where we often had our dinner. It was a very romantic place in the moonlight, with palm trees below along the beach, making a perfect setting, if only it had not been for the threat of war hanging over all our heads. There was so much talk of the Japanese attacking Malaya, but the general opinion was they would have little chance against the defences.

Roper came back whenever he could, and quite often the Dukes came over for weekends, and Yvonne on her own to spend the day with me and the children. They adored it there and were almost as brown as the Malays. Mark used our little boat and got quite good at paddling about on his own. One morning the tide, which went out at least a mile, turned rather quickly and he was cut off from the beach. I had Rory with me, so I signalled to Mark to paddle the boat parallel with the shore, thinking there would soon be a channel where he could bring it in. However, there wasn't, and by the time we had gone at least a mile – I had to put Rory on my hip and he was quite heavy at two and a half – I was very hot and worried. Eventually we found a place he could almost get in, and we were able to pull the boat up. We left it there and then had to walk all the way back to the house with everyone cross and tired, and Betty and the Malays worried stiff.

Betty was pregnant. Thinking we were leaving, she had decided it would be a good time, but of course was now beginning to wonder. Yvonne was the same way and their dates almost identical, sometime around the second week of December. Peter was offered a quarter, so we urged them to take it as our plans were uncertain, and Betty reluctantly went. By this time Roper had passed out first from both his OCTUs and was about to get his commission, which he duly did, not long before the fatal day of 8 December.

We had one amusing incident before this when we were asked to dinner at Admiralty House at the naval base, by Admiral Sir Geoffrey and Lady Layton who were friends of Roper's uncle and had been asked to be kind to us. Roper was still a private, and if he left the Changi area, had to wear uniform. I rang Lady Layton and explained this, but she said she did not mind mixing a private with General Percival, the only other soldier asked. We arrived in our open car and I got out, and Roper – taken for my driver – was told where to go and park. As I said 'good evening' to our hosts, I explained that my DRIVER was also my husband. The Admiral thought this a huge joke, and obviously had forgotten even if his wife had remembered to warn him, and insisted on taking him off directly he arrived on the scene to introduce him to the General. The highest and the lowest. Roper was not too sure if General Percival, who was not renowned for his sense of humour, really appreciated the situation as much as Sir Geoffrey. However, we had a wonderful dinner party, dining outside on the lawn.

Soon after this things happened fast. Roper got his commission and joined the regiment, coming back occasionally to sleep. The evening of 8 December was one of those perfect, moonlit, star-spangled nights. I had had my dinner alone outside and gone to bed, when I woke to hear the voices of the Malays below my window. I looked out and asked if there was something wrong. Sarleh replied there were many aeroplanes in the sky and a lot of ack-ack fire coming from Singapore town fifteen miles away (though a lot less as the crow flies). We discussed, when I got outside, what was happening. Maybe it was just a practice with our own planes, but way down I had that awful sinking feeling that at last this was IT. In the end, as the planes had passed high over our heads and all had quietened down, I persuaded them all back to bed saying tomorrow we would know if they were Jap planes. I had asked a Chinese lorry driver (we were not on the telephone) to come and collect us if the Japanese DID attack as Roper, and everyone else, felt the coast was the least safe place to be.

The next morning when I was trying to get some news out of our hopeless wireless, the Chinese lorry driver turned up. *He* was full of rumours, but the one definite thing I got out of him was that the town HAD been attacked by Japs the night before. The Malays urged me to take the children into Singapore, and they would stay and look after everything, and if things got too hot for them they promised to go back to their kampong at Serangoon where they had a house. After Betty left I had employed a Eurasian girl, Edith, to help Norsiah with the children, so she and the girls (in tears) packed, and we put as much as we could in the lorry, including our best bits of furniture, and the rest in the car.

I knew that the Cherrys would be expecting me at Abbotsford, as they had insisted that if anything happened, I was to go there. I hated leaving the Sarleh family and it was the last time I was to see any of them for some years and, sensing this, we were all in tears.

Both the Cherrys were out when we arrived – Ah-Mo came with us – so we installed ourselves and the children, both slightly bewildered by the sudden upheaval, but quite pleased to be back in their old haunts. After they were in bed that night, the Cherrys and I got together in what had been our old dressing-room which they had made into a sitting-room as it was easy to 'black out' and was air conditioned. We discussed the situation and the terrible disaster of Pearl Harbour, and decided there was nothing to be done meantime. Roper rang and said the regiment were going out to their WAR position at Panarang on the Johore mainland, and he was relieved that we were installed in Abbotsford.

Mrs Cherry was back at the hospital, and he at the office all day. I got in touch with a great friend, Mary Brooke, who, with a new baby, was sitting waiting like all of us. Two days went by and the anticipated air raids never came, though there were planes overhead often during the night. We kept the doors in the bedrooms open and only used a torch, so after 6.30 p.m. everything was slightly nerve-racking with no lights. Then the third evening after dinner, when we were sitting listening to the wireless, came the shattering new of the sinking of the *Prince of Wales* and the *Repulse* battleships. It seemed unbelievable, these were our two great stand-bys. Furthermore, from the personal angle, Dick Beckwith, an old friend of Instow days (and later when he had visited us in Singapore on his way to China), was on board the *Prince of Wales* as the Gunnery Officer.

I went to bed very depressed, but was wakened by Mrs Cherry at midnight to say there was someone on the telephone urgently wanting to speak to me. This was Dick. I could not believe it. He said quite a lot of them had been saved and were back at the naval base. they were not to be allowed into Singapore for security reasons, so could I go out the next day with anything I could get hold of in the way of clothes, etc. I promised to do what I could, and rang Mary Brooke at 6.30 a.m. to ask her to come with me. Luckily we had a pass into the naval base, as we had quite often visited a naval bachelor friend there. This enabled Mary and to get in with only a bit of banter with the guard. I suppose it was a historic occasion as we were the first females (and rescuers) these men had seen.

Dick and the others we met were all pretty badly shaken by what had happened, but more than grateful for the few things we had managed to take them. Dick urged us both to 'get away' as soon as we could, and not to wait for the general evacuation which he felt was bound to come. Obviously he felt, like all the others, that if the Japs could sink two ships like this, what would they do to the town of Singapore? We were not allowed to stay long, but it certainly gave us a lot to discuss on the way back. Roper and I had always agreed that once the Japs landed on Malayan soil, it would be best for me to take the boys to some safe place but not too far away.

The next day I was visited by Aubrey Wallich, the friend in the firm who had lived in our East Coast Road house, who agreed with Dick's advice. And then our great friend Robbie, of the Argylls [regiment] (whom we had known with his wife, Dor, before the war, and who had come back to Singapore on the staff of Duff-Cooper), turned up with the same advice. By this time the Japs had landed up on the East coast near the Siamese border – at Tumput, a place we knew well, where we had spent a memorable holiday with the Robertsons, staying with Roper's brother who was stationed there in one of the Boustead 'outposts'. We had spent two weeks snipe shooting, and bathing on the lovely beach of 'Passionate Love', where the Japs made their first landing. Robbie and I had a long nostalgic talk about all this over a bottle of champagne he had brought with him. It was the last time I ever saw him, as later he was killed fighting up-country when he had taken over command of the Argylls.

I made up my mind then that I should leave, and managed to get a message out to Roper to ring me. This he did, and agreed the best thing I could do was to try and get on a boat to Calcutta. I rang Bourstead's shipping department, and was told there was a cargo ship with passenger accommodation for twelve leaving the following Monday. It was Thursday, 11 December, so I said to book me two double cabins. I would have liked to take 'Ah-Mo' with me instead of the rather neurotic Edith – though she was keen to come – but when I asked him, he said he could not come as he had two small children being fostered by a relation as his wife was in China, and he felt he could not leave them. I was somewhat surprised, as we had thought him a bachelor, but naturally in these circumstances he was right to stay. So I told Edith to go home and ask her parents for advice, and she returned saying they were quite happy at her going with me. She, I felt, would at least be a pair of hands and someone I could leave with the children, if things were difficult.

Roper had managed to arrange to come in and say goodbye on the Sunday. Both the Cherrys thought I was doing the right thing but before they got home on the Friday evening, I was rung by the office to say that the ship we were booked on had come in early and was now sailing the next day instead of Monday. Did I still want my passage? If not, there was a queue of people who did. I was a bit taken aback, and asked for time to think it over. 'All right,' the girl said, 'I'll give you five minutes.' This was one of the worst decisions I ever had to make. I knew it meant I might not see Roper (ever?) again, and yet it was the best chance I might get to take the boys away to safety in some kind of normality, plus quite a lot of our possessions. I made up my mind that we had to go, and rang her back to say so. I then rang Mary and told her what I had decided to do. If it had not been for the fact that Charles, her husband, was still going to the office and coming home to sleep each night, she might have come with me, but she had two older boys at school in England, so naturally if she had to go anywhere, felt she must go back to them. She said she would come over and help me to pack. We were still at it by midnight. We were exhausted, but helped by finding among the things I had brought from Tanah Marah, a case of champagne, so we kept ourselves bolstered up with a bottle or two.

We had a tearful farewell and I slept until 6.00 a.m. and then was up getting ourselves organised to leave soon after breakfast. I sadly said farewell to Ada and Rob Cherry who had been so understanding and helpful to us, and they both departed before us. More tears with some of the staff who had assembled to wish us luck, and then suddenly out-of-the-blue, Harry Roper-Caldbeck (Roper's brother) arrived, wearing, to the boys' delight, a tin helmet camouflaged with bits of leaves and bamboo. I asked how on earth he had heard we were off two days early, and though he was in the volunteers and out on the West Coast, word had come through the grapevine and he had got leave to come and help us.

I had not even managed to get through to Roper to tell him our change of plans, so was doubly thankful to see Harry and knew he would explain everything when they next met. He drove our car, and just as we were passing the cold storage, he said, 'Isn't your fur coat in there?' It was, but it had not even occurred to me to get it out, or even that it was possible. However, Harry emerged with it after only a few minutes, helped no doubt by the firm's connection with the S. C. S. Company. It was typical of Harry to be so thoughtful, and I was more than grateful, particularly by having him see us installed on board.

It was a nice clean ship and we had two deck cabins, so Edith and Rory went in one and Mark and I in the other. They were nice and cool at night, but in order to be certain we showed no light, the bulbs were taken out. We were allowed to use a torch with discretion, but in the week it took to get to Calcutta I broke three thermoses in the night. There was a pretty mixed crowd of passengers, and after dinner some of us stayed on in the saloon and played cards, which helped to pass the time as dinner was at 7.00 p.m. soon after dark. Edith preferred to go to bed or sit on deck, so would keep guard until I went up myself around 10.00 p.m.

It was very hot during the day but the children were quite happy, and the sailors as usual very good with them and often put the hose on them, much to their delight, when they were cleaning the deck down. Everything appeared very normal, and we kept off the main shipping routes to avoid any Jap submarines that might be lurking. Sometimes at night on deck it sounded *exactly* like aeroplanes approaching in the distance, but we never saw any and the Captain said it was only the wind in the rigging that gave the illusion, but I was not sure if this was not just to stop the women getting panicky. I felt very much out on a limb, not knowing where I was going to eventually land up, or what the future held, and feeling pretty desperate about having to leave without seeing Roper. In some ways I realised it was probably less heart-breaking for both of us to be spared the agony of saying goodbye, and the children were really too young to understand the implication involved. I had told them we were going on a holiday, and to get away from the Japanese who might kill us with their bombs if we stayed in Singapore. They knew that their father would 'soon beat them off' and then we could return to Singapore.

When we reached Calcutta I was met by a man in a firm which Bousteads did business with, and who Rob Cherry had asked to look after us. The Chairman and his wife were away, so he, a bachelor, had been detailed off to do the job. Quite obviously he did not want to get involved, so after handing me some money and saying he had booked us into a hotel, he departed, never to be seen again. Luckily there was an army officer who had come on board, and as I was the only 'army wife', he help me get ashore and through all the usual customs and passport people. It was boiling hot and quite a walk to the taxi when we were eventually ready to leave.

The hotel was one of those huge, white stone buildings, very cool and with an enormous, nearly empty dining-room, where we were waited on by Indian waiters, beautifully dressed in white with red turbans and sashes. But the garden was small, and I had to hire a taxi to take the children out to the botanical gardens in the evening to play. I stuck it for two days without seeing anyone I knew, and soon realised that I would have to do something as we could not go on for long as we were. I suddenly had a brainwave that some friends of Joan's who I also knew quite well, Joan and Maurice Yates, had moved to Calcutta from Singapore about a year previously. I feverishly looked them up in the telephone book, and to my delight found them in. When I rang them they could not have been kinder, and insisted there and then on fetching us and taking us to stay at their house.

Never had I felt more relieved to be among friends. They had one son of twelve who was up in Darjeeling at school and a marvellous big garden, and were both so sweet to us all. The house was two-storey, but divided into two. They had the lower part, and some people who were away on local leave in Ceylon had the upper. Maurice cabled them for permission for us to use it for the two months they were to be away. They answered 'of course' so we moved in. This really saved our lives, and we were able to lead a more or less normal life again.

Part Three
South African Diary

Cape Town 1942

WHEN WE FIRST ARRIVED in the Cape we stayed at a hotel in Camps Bay, a small place about eight miles from the city, on the Atlantic side of the bay. My mother and Charles had been living there for a year after retiring from Malaya. It was good to find an anchorage after wandering for five months. Staying with friends in Calcutta, we went through the agonizing time of listening to unreliable reports and rumours from Singapore, with only one personal contact of a letter written in mid-December by Roper, saying his regiment, The Gordon Highlanders, were back in Singapore after retreating down the peninsula, and that they were now preparing to defend the Island. Then a Christmas parcel arrived for the children, and after that silence. Singapore duly fell to the Japanese, so I decided to go down to Bombay (a two day journey by train). I might get some information there from women arriving on the evacuation boats. I scanned the list for familiar names, and thought I had traced Betty Webber, but it turned out to be someone else. I put our names down for a passage to Cape Town, but then could do nothing but wait. We spent every day at Breach Kandy, a swimming club a few miles along the coast reached by bus. One day there I met two young officers who we had known in Singapore, and who had escaped two days before it fell. One of them had seen Roper in Tanglin Club the week before, so it was something to know he was still alive then. Stories were coming out all the time, but no official news. They had heard that some of the regiments were interned in their own barracks, and in that case the Gordons would be at Changi, so one could only pray that if he was not dead or wounded, Roper was with them.

When I was in Calcutta I had met a girl called Norah Wade. She was a 'blonde bombshell' with startlingly beautiful green eyes and short-cut naturally curly hair. She had left her husband, and was living with a rather nice 'older man' who she said was her guardian. She wanted to get to Cape Town and asked me if she could travel with us and help with the children. This seemed a good idea at the time, as Edith, the girl I had taken with us from Singapore, had decided that she would prefer to stay behind in Calcutta. She could get a job in the hospital there, and seemed quite confident that she would be allowed to go back to Singapore, and that being a Eurasian she would not be interned. Norah turned out to be rather a dead-loss, as the moment we got to Bombay, although sharing rooms in a boarding house with us, she departed every day on business of her own. She apparently had a Canadian man who had been detailed off to look after her by her 'guardian'. Later this man had to go off on a business trip and offered us his very smart flat and servants for the three weeks he was away. We jumped at it, as it was very close to Breach Kandy, and the boarding house was pretty awful and very hot. He suggested that the boys might enjoy seeing his plane take off, and also that if we went out before he left he could show us around. He seemed as startled as I was when we met; he was young and good looking, when I had imagined him old and fat, and Lord knows what picture Norah had painted of me.

After that Norah started to come with us to Breach Kandy, but she was always surrounded by a crowd of eager young men, so we did not see much of her. After three weeks we were told we had berths on an ancient Anchor Line ship sailing non-stop to Cape Town. We said farewell to the Indian cook and boy who had looked after us so well, and I put up prayers to the nameless (to me) Canadian who had so kindly come to our rescue, and went on board to find we had been allotted two two-berth cabins. They were small and boiling hot as the portholes were firmly sealed because of the blackout. Norah soon found accommodation elsewhere. She told me she objected to the fact that I had asked her not to smack the boys, and therefore could not control them. As I had only asked her to sleep with one of them, this was obviously nonsense, and the real reason was that the ship's doctor, who had immediately become enamoured with her charms, had offered her his cabin on the deck, so from that time on I saw little of her.

I made friends with a woman called Ann Myers who, leaving her husband in Bombay – he was Editor of *The Times* – was taking her two girls, Edna and Carmel, to the better schools and climate of South Africa. They were both quite a bit older than the boys, but so sweet with them, spending hours entertaining them, and generally keeping an eye on them, when I washed and ironed, etc. The worst time was at nights after the children were in bed. I would sit and read a book or play cards with Ann in the dining-room, as it was on the same level as the cabins and within hearing distance. I was never parted from three life-jackets and a little leather sling bag – which I still have – containing all I could cram into it, in case we were torpedoed. People have often asked me since what I put into it. I can remember most things. A five pound note, aspirin, sunburn cream, three scarfs for our heads, boiled sweets and chocolate – which melted every day – a lipstick and comb (I was only twenty-seven) and some playing cards.

I found myself appointed unofficial baby-sitter by other mothers, who seemed to want to spend their time up on the top deck spooning with the officers, or any lone male passengers whom they had picked up. It was not that I was being self righteous, but apart from having no inclinations that way, I felt the whole object of my leaving Roper was to look after our children properly. On one occasion I heard wails coming from a nearby cabin, and on going to investigate, found the small boy in question had plastered himself and the bed-clothes with his mother's make-up. He was kept in by a 'pig-net' but had managed to get his hands through to the dressing table. The mess was indescribable. His little sister on the top bunk said, 'Send for Mummy,' so I did. After a few nights of trying to cope with the heat, and changing the vests the boys slept in, at least three times, I decided to try sleeping on deck. This was a disaster, as the noise of people talking, laughing, and even playing the guitar, made sleep impossible before midnight. So the next night I put our mattresses out of our porthole onto the little deck which ran

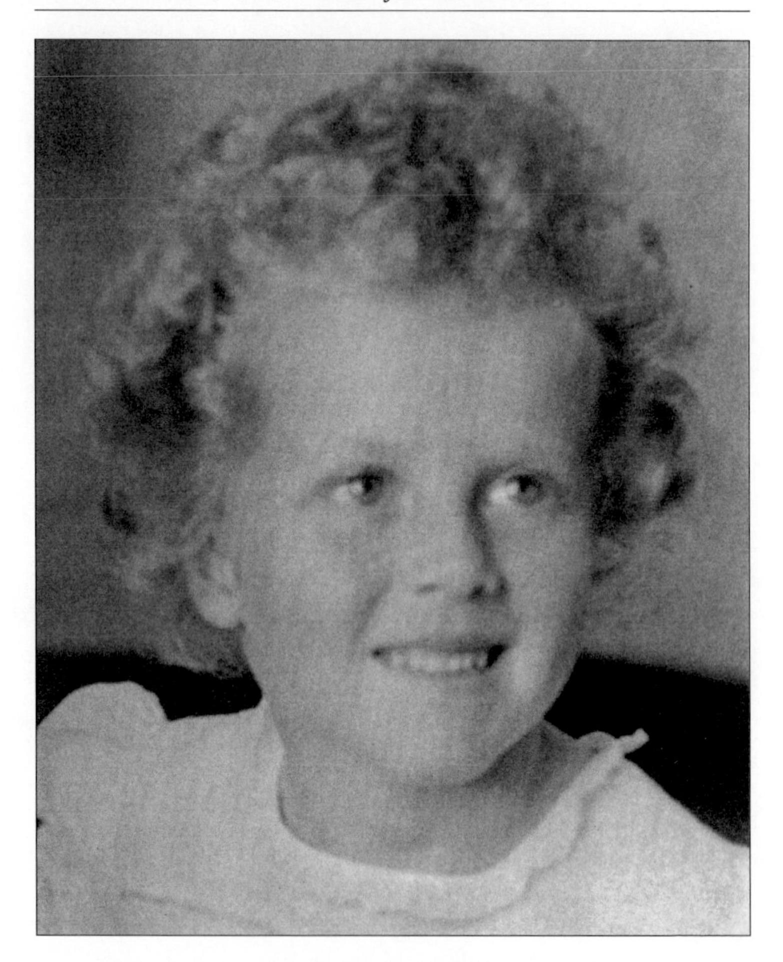

Jane, Jack's daughter

alongside the cabin. It was so narrow that there was only a tiny space beyond the mattress on the sea side of the deck, just wide enough for someone to get past. I had to go to bed with the children as it was only too easy for them to climb the rail and fall overboard. It worked well at first, and it was heaven to be cool, and the boys went out like a light each night. Then we had a major upset. One of the officers must have trodden on Rory's little finger hanging over the side of the mattress. I woke to piercing screams and the retreating figure of a man's back. I took them both inside to the light and found Rory's finger squashed to the bone. The doctor – called no doubt from more enjoyable duties – could do nothing but bind it up, and forbid me to sleep on the deck again.

It took three weeks to get to Cape Town, so finally when I saw my mother and Charles waiting on the quayside to greet us, it seemed like a miracle. The last seen of Norah was of her being carried off on a stretcher. She had apparently contacted some bug and had a septic leg. Presumably the ministration of the doctor had failed, but she told me that during the voyage she had received three proposals of marriage. This was later when my conscience pricked me, and I paid her a visit in a nursing home run by Irish nuns. They greeted me with cries of 'You have come to see our darling Norah, such a saint she is to be sure.' To be sure, I thought.

My mother had booked us into the Marine Hotel in Camps Bay where she and Charles were living in a small flat on the sea front. They were so good about looking after the boys, so I could go into the town and visit the house agents, as I felt the sooner we were settled in a house the better.

I even managed a 'night out' at the Kelvin Grove Club. Jim Young, an American who had been on the ship and who I had played deck tennis with occasionally, rang me to ask if I would go out to a party with him. I told him that it sounded fun, but, like Cinderella, I would have to leave at midnight. The couple who ran the hotel had volunteered to look after the children, and they were perfectly happy at being left and almost asleep anyway. We had a good time and Jim made no protest about being dragged away, as he was leaving for the States early in the morning.

We saw Mummy and Charles every day and they often had Jane, my brother Jack's little girl, with them. She was six months younger than Mark, but had been so upset at being parted from her father, who she adored, that she was literally struck dumb. She did occasionally speak to Mummy, but remained completely silent with us. Trudy, her mother, was living at Seapoint along the coast towards Cape Town. She was pregnant, and had had no news of Jack; he had been, like Harry, Roper's brother, in the Volunteers in Singapore.

We heard there was a house to let on the road that led from

the bay up to Kloof-Nak at the bottom of Table Mountain. It had a wonderful view over the sea and the mountain behind, and was the last house in a row with open country at the back. I liked it immediately, and it had good accommodation on the floor, three bedrooms and servant's room at the back. I went to the agents to say I would take it, and was slightly taken back by their reluctance at dealing with a woman, asking for my husband's signature. I explained why this was impossible, and assured them that I WAS in the position to pay the rent, etc. and eventually they agreed! I soon realised that women in South Africa had a long way to go before they were 'liberated'. After this things began to move rapidly. Ann Myers asked if she could come and share the house with us for a few weeks before she went up to Johannesburg. It meant her having to sleep in the sitting-room or with the girls, as two bedrooms were doubles, but mine at the back was very small. Then a very nice woman appeared in answer to my advertisement for a maid, bringing with her a Zulu girl called Virginia. She told me she was 'a treasure' and was only parting with her because she was going away. Virginia was mission-trained and a Catholic, a tall, jolly girl who really was the treasure she was said to be. She loved the boys, and they her, worked like a Trojan, was always cheerful and bright, and forgot to go out on her days off.

I thought a large dog would complete our household, and heard of a Great Dane bull-mastiff cross, a year old. He had been left at some kennels while his owner had had to go off on business, but he now sent word that he would not be returning to the Cape, so would they find him a good home. I liked the look of him, he was brindle and called Zulu, so I said I would take him on a week's trial. He walked into the house as if he owned it, licked the children, and then settled down on the sofa. I thought this is 'now or never' if I am going to be in control, so I ordered him off and he growled at me. Inwardly quaking, I got him by the collar and pulled him off. He, luckily, accepted the fact that I was master, and from then on I had no trouble, though Ann and Virginia were both a bit nervous of him. All the same they both realised that a large and fierce-looking dog was quite an asset. There were a lot of hair-raising stories going round. The local white South African women whose husbands

Mark and Zulu

Below: *Author and Zulu at Camps Bay, Cape Town*

were at war, slept with pistols under their pillows and were too frightened to let their children out of the garden on their own. Both Ann and I, brought up in Malaya and India, found their attitude difficult to take, and we allowed the children to go for walks on their own, and make 'camps' up at the back. Occasionally they came back and reported that a black man had spoken to them, but they were all perfectly friendly and unfrightening. There was a native village up above us, and the children belonging there had to pass our house coming and going to school. They pretended to be terrified of Zulu and screamed even before he had so much as looked at them. They excited him into barking at them, but he never went down the steps onto the road, so it ended up in being more of a game on both sides.

There was a very nice English family called Short, who lived just up the road on the other side and on the top of some steps – there were over a hundred – which led down to the coast road, and across to a small natural swimming pool in the rocks. We all went there at weekends when the main bay got very crowded. Phyll Short had two children, Diana and Quinney, both older than the boys but still young enough for them all to get on well together. Phyll's husband was in oil in the Persian Gulf, and she was there for a break and to see about suitable boarding schools for Quinney. One day she and Ann went into town, leaving me in charge of the six children. We decided to build a hut in our garden. Standing on a ladder and knocking a post in with the wrong side of an axe, I came down onto Edna's head instead of the post. Blood spurted, but she seemed quite unconcerned as I rushed her into the bathroom and under the cold tap. The rest of the children crowding round gaping at the exciting sight of so much blood. Thank God it soon stopped and I was able to cut some hair away and put on a plaster. I was slightly unnerved though by Ann, who on her return, seeing her daughter and hearing the story in different versions from several age groups, rounded on me for not calling a doctor.

Another family we got to know well were the Northys from the Seychelles. They lived at the bottom of the hill behind the bay. The boy, Vernon, was seventeen, and his sister, Amathe, thirteen. Mrs Northy was older than me and a very sweet and understanding woman. The children went to day school in Cape Town, but at the weekends spent most of their time with all of us. Vernon suggested that if I bought an old rowboat he and his friend Bob (one of the English twins we got to know later), would do it up for us. They brought it up into our garage and spent a lot of time on it. I was ragged by Ann and Phyll that he had an infatuation for me, as well as boat building. I suppose he was just at the age that a girl of twenty-seven seemed to him like 'a woman of the world', though it was the last thing I thought of myself.

We went for long walks with Zulu and the Shorts' red setter and discovered a beautiful glen not far from the house. It was sheltered from the winds which often made the beach impossible, and had a clear, fast running stream through it. One day the boys and I traced this up to the road above the house about a mile away. It came down the mountains in a gushing rush of water to a large pool before going under the road through a concrete pipe. The boys were dropping sticks into the pool, when one of the dogs brushed against Rory's legs, pushing him in, where he sank like a stone. I had ghastly visions of him disappearing under the road and getting stuck in the pipe so leapt after him. I managed to grab him as he came up, but the sides were sheer concrete and I could only get a grip with one hand. Mark kept his head, luckily, and pulled Rory up and out of my arms, and so I was able to get myself out too. We ran for home and were none the worse for the adventure.

I was very upset at receiving a cable from the War Office stating that Roper was posted missing from 15 December. Soon afterwards I had a letter from Yvonne Duke, who had got to Durban with her baby, and was staying with an aunt. She said to take little notice of the cable, as ALL the regular officers' wives who had left their husbands in Singapore, had received the same message, and it was routine in such cases.

I was thankful for Zulu sleeping beside me, when one night I woke to hear footsteps outside my bedroom window. Without putting the light on I looked out – there were bars over the window but it was open – and I could see a figure in the moonlight. I called out, 'Who is it?' and the two men – Black – turned and ran out of the back gate which led onto the common, or velt. Zulu went mad but I dared not let him out. Ann woke up, and then Virginia appeared out of her room which was at the back, but separate from the main house. She said they were 'bad men' and that they had been trying her door (which she kept locked) for the obvious reason, and so were probably not trying to burgle us. I reported it to the police the next day, and they rather agreed with her theory, as apparently so many of the local maids were only too willing.

Soon after this the Myers left, and I had a letter from Betty Bishop. She and Valerie, her baby, born a few days after Yvonne's Bridget, had got to Bombay and we had only just missed them. They had then gone up to Quetta with a family who wanted help with one small girl. She said the moment things looked a bit safer on the seas, she hoped to come and join us. Yvonne had mentioned doing the same thing, as she apparently was not too happy living with the aunt. I wrote and suggested she came until Betty arrived, which would obviously not be for some time. There was not room in the house for all of us, but we could settle that when the time came.

Zulu amused us by standing for hours in the shallow pools and watching, fascinated, the numerous small fish swimming about, which he would then make a dart at, but without ever any success. Rory was more expert, and would also spend hours standing on the rocks by the open sea and often catching small fish with the aid of dried octopus, the perfect bait. Vernon and his friends were all mad keen on the sport of 'octopus catching'. They put their bare arms under the rocks and pools left by the outgoing tide. The creatures then wrapped themselves round the proffered arm, and when they had a good hold, the boys gave a heave and pulled them away onto the sand. I was horrified when I first saw it happen, thinking they would be marked for life by the suckers, but in actual fact these impressed the skin for a very short time, and had no after effect. They would peel them off, turn them inside out, and hang them up in a tree to dry: certainly the most effective bait. I never let Rory fish like this on his own. Sometimes the waves were huge, and one day he gently slipped off the rock he was standing on, but I managed to grab him by the hair before he disappeared. The local small boys of six and seven years old were really tough. They thought nothing of going out to sea in their little home-made corrugated iron canoes and surfing back to the shore. As there was some considerable danger from sharks in the open sea, I was amazed that their parents allowed this, particularly as two boys had been taken at the next bay since we had been there. Anyway, the open sea – the Atlantic – was always ice-cold even in high summer, but the rock pools were warm. It was still then only early spring, and the wind blew very strongly from the sea at least three days out of seven. Then the beach was impossible, with the sand blowing up into one's eyes, so we spent our time inland. Some of the country behind our houses and upon the mountain was fascinating, and we went for long walks, and soon the spring flowers were appearing. Carpets of them when the sun was out. It was hot during the day, but quite cold at nights.

I gradually managed to buy bits of furniture to replace the rather awful hired stuff I had taken over with the house. I made new curtains with Mummy's help, and began to feel the place looked something like home. The children were settled and happy, and with the money I had got out of Singapore and my Captain's pay, I could cope if I was careful. I would have liked a car, but Charles was very generous at lending me his, so I felt it was an unnecessary expense. The Onions, Mary and Dick, who I had made friends with from the hotel where they were staying on local leave from Rhodesia, often took me out to dine and to the cinema, or theatre, in Cape Town. I felt quite happy about leaving the boys with Virginia and Zulu to guard them.

The news continued to be depressing and a lot of the local people lost people at Tobruk. Convoys were coming in on their way to the Middle East and the troops swarmed everywhere. We took some of them back to our home for baths and a meal (much to the boys' delight), but they were wonderfully looked-after in Cape Town and all the local women went overboard to entertain them. Yet we, as refugees, were never asked into any of their houses, which rather amazed me. I had not been there nearly as long as Mummy and Charles, and as I had the children I was unable to help with any war work, but both of them had met most of the inhabitants of Camps Bay through working with them on various volunteer jobs, but even they did not get invited to their houses. We never did discover the reason for this, and it seemed to apply to all the *women* who, through the war, found themselves exiled from their own homes and country. Yet, with the forces, they gained the reputation of being the most hospitable people in the world.

I had a letter from Roper's mother saying she had heard in some roundabout, but authentic, way that he was definitely a prisoner and with the Regiment in Changi. The relief in getting this news was tremendous, although it shattered any dreams I had of him, having escaped, turning up out of the blue. The main thing was that he was alive, and I rushed down to my mother with the news. Mrs Northy had also heard her husband was safe in Batavia and the Dutch Consul had informed her that she would now be allowed to write, and apparently the same applied to other POWs wherever they were held. Vernon came up to finish off the boat, and because we all felt happier there was a good deal of ragging with the brushes, and paint flying, mush to the boys' delight.

My poor mother, who was desperately worried as no news had yet come through about my brother, Jack, suddenly looked very ill and tired, and was ordered to bed for a complete rest. Her blood pressure was high, but the doctor seemed to think there was nothing else wrong. We had a birthday party for Jane in our house as Mummy was not up to it. Trudy's baby was not due for some time, but she had engaged a Nanny and Jane seemed happier and was taken out for walks, but she was still desperately shy and unable to talk to us. All the same she seemed to enjoy the party and our presents. My friends, the Onions, were there but just about to go back to Rhodesia with Robin, who was the same age as Mark and they had become great friends, as I had with his parents, whom I knew I would miss a lot. Mary said she hoped to be back the following year.

We launched the boat the next morning with due ceremony, and it seemed to hold all the children without turning over, as it had a flat bottom. The same morning there were a lot of penguins on the beach. They were covered in oil as apparently a tanker had gone on the rocks not far away. But it was a mystery how they came to be washed ashore as the nearest breeding ground was over forty miles away. Amathe and I took some of them home to try and get the oil off, but only one survived. Vernon had left school and was hoping for a job in a bank. He had tried for the army but had been turned down on his medical.

He obviously was not physically very strong, and was deeply upset about it.

Roper's mother had hinted that his brother, Noel, could possibly turn up in Cape Town *en route* to the Middle East with his regiment, the Black Watch. He was a regular soldier, so as every convoy arrived we had high hopes of seeing him. All the same I could not believe it when one day he appeared on the doorstep. Of course both the boys decided to have temperatures and were in their beds. So disappointing for them as he was marvellous with children, and had the extra glamour of being a real soldier and their father's brother. Still, they were not so ill that they could not enjoy him. Mummy, who was quite recovered, came up to be with them so I could go in and meet him in the car the following day. We shopped and bought presents to send home to his family, and he also got toys for the boys and we drove out so he could give them himself, and say goodbye. He and I had a tearful farewell at the gates of the docks where I dropped him. He was off early the next morning, and we both felt that we were the last links with home.

We were told that we were to be allowed to send a 'personal clothing and medical' parcel to POWs in the Far East. It was not a regular service, but a 'special opportunity' arranged through Lourenço Marques. Mummy and I went in to do the shopping, while the boys spent the day with the Shorts. We bought things to send to Roper and his brother, and my brother Jack. We spent about eleven pounds on each, but it was difficult to get the right sizes, as stocks were low. Still it seemed worthwhile as the general opinion was that they were more likely to arrive when sent through a diplomatic ship, than via Geneva. The convoys going East all sailed past the house, and presented a magnificent sight. The sea was still very rough owing to the everlasting wind, with great waves blowing up in sheets of spray over the escorting destroyers. I thought to myself it was probably better viewed from the vantage point of dry land. Some of the soldiers I met had told me that it was their first time ever at sea, and they had felt sick and miserable all the way out to the Cape, so I wondered how Noel and his Jocks were faring?

My next door neighbours, the Stinsons, consisted of father and son, and a very glamorous blonde, who was his second wife. I sometimes saw Mr Stinson in the garden, but we were only on nodding acquaintance, although he always appeared quite friendly. I was therefore a bit upset when Vernon told me that young Stinson – who was about his age, only looked much older – had said they considered Zulu a 'damned nuisance, and he should be put down'. Vernon had apparently hotly defended me – and Zulu – by saying that, as I had no man to protect me, it was quite right in my keeping a large dog. He was perfectly harmless, and only got excited and barked when the coloured children came past the house at school time. The parents of these had complained to the police, who came to see me about it. I explained the position and I heard no more from either. He *did* have one bad habit which I found it difficult to break him of, and that was bullying small dogs he met on the beach. He would sit on them, and although they did not get hurt, naturally the irate owners thought they were being killed. I would pull him off and the dog in question would emerge shaking itself and none the worse, with the owners then turning on *me* at owning such a terrible monster.

Charles did some night volunteer police work, and on those evenings he would drop Mummy off to have supper with me. One night, when Virginia was bringing in the food which eaten in front of the fire, she announced first that she had caught a canary that had been singing in the garden all day and intended to buy a cage for it and present it to the boys. And, secondly, which made my heart sink, was that her boyfriend had appeared from Johannesburg that day. 'Just for a visit,' she said, but she seemed very excited and I wondered if marriage was in the air. To my horror she announced in a few days' time that he was going to marry her and, even worse, take her back to Johannesburg when his leave was up in *three* weeks' time. Poor Virginia, she assured me that really she would much prefer to stay with us, but if she refused him this time he might not come back again. She was also worried, she said, that if she did not get married and have lots of children, there would be no one to look after her in her old age. So I had to resign myself to losing the 'treasure' though she insisted she had a friend, just as good, called Gertie who would come instead. We attended the wedding ceremony, though not the reception, and Virginia was a marvellous sight in a long white satin dress with a tulle veil over her large, smiling, black face. We felt so sad at losing her as we had really become very attached to her delightful, gay personality. Gertie, who turned out to have a small boy who had not been mentioned until she arrived, was large and fat, and although quite nice, was not a patch on Virginia. Also her child was totally unhousetrained, and would stand and pee, to my horror, in the middle of the kitchen floor! Still, she was kind, and I could trust her with the children if I wanted to go out at nights. She would settle herself, and child, on the floor in front of the fire in the sitting-room and remain there until I got home.

I had found a poor lost stray dog in the town and, after registering it with the police, brought it home with me. It was a shaggy, small brown bitch, and Zulu never turned a hair, but I realised I would have to try and find it a home. I kept it for three weeks, then heard of a family who wanted a bitch, and in the end she went to them and was a great success.

One night our boat was stolen from the beach, but Vernon said that he and the twins, Bob and Ken, would make us another if I provided the material. We all got the 'Kreefing' bug. This was the sport of trying to catch crayfish from the very deep rock pools. You threaded a necklace of mussels onto a bit of wire, attaching this to a line; then dropped this down to the bottom of the pool, hoping the crayfish would come out of its hole and attach itself to the bait. You would then very carefully and slowly pull it up so someone could net it. Half the time it would let go, and sink before the person with the net was within striking distance. Still, we caught quite a lot, and they were very good to eat; even the children liked them.

Trudy's baby, a boy, John, was born without much trouble. It was so sad for her still with no news whatsoever of Jack, but she was delighted it was a boy, and Jane pleased with a brother.

Mummy and Charles and I had a good weep at a film called *Mrs Miniver* with Walter Pidgeon and Greer Garson, which portrayed a typical wartime family living in a country village in England with the husband away, but occasionally returning. (Lucky girl, I thought.)

The Myers returned from Johannesburg and stayed for a bit, then I heard that Yvonne and Bridget definitely wanted to come until Betty and Valerie arrived. The Myers girls were going to boarding school anyway, and Ann hoped to get back to India. I said I would do all I could about having them on their days out, etc., but it would not be easy during the holidays. Yvonne had written that she hoped to arrive at the beginning of November, and Ann seemed to think once the girls were safely in school, she would go to a hotel in Seapoint and wait for her passage.

A friend from Malaya, Anita Knight, rang me with some news. First, she had heard that her husband, Leonard, a police officer, was definitely alive and well, and in the Changi prison. She also had a story about a man who had escaped from Singapore and walked right through Malaya to Siam where he was now hiding. He seemed to know that a lot of the British Army prisoners had been sent up to jungle camps there, and were quite well treated. How the message had got out, nobody knew. Still it was something to cling on to. Anita said she was giving a party to celebrate the news about Leonard and would I go? I gladly accepted, as although I was as content as I could be without Roper and certainly did not crave for the bright lights, it was good to occasionally get away from the children and enjoy a mixed party. She said she had asked some naval officers she knew who were on leave from destroyer duty, and she suggested I spent the night with her as she lived much nearer the town.

Mrs Northy told me that the twins' sister, Doff Barton, who I had only just met, was starting a nursery school and would I be interested? She was a very sweet English girl married to a South African-Norwegian called Sven. She had brought her two young twin brothers out to South Africa at the beginning of the war, as Sven and she lived and worked in the Cape. She had worked with young children before she was married and had the reputation of being very good with them. The boys certainly took to her when I went along to see her. They lived in an old, very large disused youth hostel, with a big garden, up at the back where most of the older houses were. They had converted one end for the schoolroom, and lived in the other half themselves. They started the following week, and I bought a bicycle and took the boys on the carrier. I found this easy enough on the way there as it was downhill and then on the flat, but it was a bit of a drag on the last bit going back and I made the boys walk while I pushed the bike. Still I enjoyed the three hours I had to myself each morning, and often went for long walks with Zulu. The boys settled down well and there was never any trouble getting them to go, and they seemed to be very fond of Doff, and she of them. There were about ten children in all and she kept them all happily occupied.

Yvonne had written to say that they would be arriving the following week. I had got a cot for Bridget and had given them the smaller bedroom, so the boys' could also be used as a playroom for them all. I was quite excited at the thought of seeing Yvonne again. It seemed ages since we were all together in Singapore. I went to meet them in Charles' car, off the train from Durban. There were masses of troops being met by their wives, but finally I found Yvonne and Bridget and we fell into each other's arms, weeping. Neither of us were very emotional people, but we had both gone through a good deal since we last saw each other. Bridget was tiny for her eight months, and had a pathetic waifish look that went to one's heart. We got back to the house, and finally all the children settled for the night, and Yvonne and I sat up talking into the small hours. We had known each other nearly all our lives, and so it was easy enough to pour out all those things that one had to bottle up. She had had a pretty ghastly time getting away from Singapore on a troopship. They were down in the hold of the ship for three days with no milk or napkins for Bridget, which obviously helped account for her frailness. Anyway, the South African sun and a normal life should help her a lot, we decided. The boys were delighted to have Bridget in the house, and remembered Yvonne quite well as she had been a frequent visitor to our house. They soon got into a routine, and Yvonne was a great help as we shared the chores and she was a good cook, and made quite a lot of 'extras' that Gertie was not capable of (or me).

Soon after she arrived was the night of Anita's party, so my mother came up to spend the evening with Yvonne, while I departed, feeling rather selfish that she was not coming too. There were eight of us. We had an excellent dinner at the Café Royal, and then on to the Star Dust Night Club which had an excellent band. This was a side of Cape Town that I hardly knew existed. We did not quite 'dance all night', but it was well after three before we got to bed, and we were up at seven as Anita had to be at her office by eight, and I got the bus out to Camps Bay and was home by eight-thirty.

After taking the boys to school and leaving Bridget asleep in her pram and guarded by Gertie, Yvonne and I often went for long walks up Table Mountain accompanied, of course, by Zulu. There was a path alongside a pipeline and parallel with the mountain top, where you got wonderful views of the sea and surroundings. We would sometimes return through the woods which led down almost to the Bartons, so we could pick up the boys. One day we had a rather nasty experience. Just near where the path started, there was a small cottage, completely on its own, housing one of the workers on the cable-car. There was a goat tethered on a bit of ground nearby. We had often seen it before and Zulu had never as much as glanced at it. This particular day the goat started going round in a circle on its tethering rope, and bleating. Zulu thought this was a game and started after it. We called him, not in the least apprehending trouble at this stage. On looking back we saw that, instead of playing, he was attacking the poor goat. We rushed to grab and pull him off, but this did not prove so easy. He had got a pretty good hold by that time. Eventually, while Yvonne held on to his hindquarters, I managed to get a hold behind his jaws

Rory, Bridget and Mark

and prise his mouth open. We pulled him away, panting with exhaustion, as he was too. I got a good grip of his collar and dragged him away; there we waited while Yvonne went off to look for help. She came back to say there was nobody around and the cottage was shut up. The goat was bleeding profusely from the throat, and we thought it would pass out at any moment. We waited for some time and then, to our amazement, the bleeding stopped and it started to graze as if nothing had happened, so we went on our way. A few weeks later when I was climbing up to the top with some experts, we had to pass the goat who had a small boy in attendance this time. I asked him if it was his goat,and was it quite fit? He answered 'Yes' to both questions, looking a bit surprised at my interest, but I thought it expedient to leave well alone.

Yvonne and I were so excited at us both getting cables on the same day to say that Dukie and Roper were both alive and well, and prisoners in Changi with the regiment in their own barracks. This came on 17 December, so was the best kind of Christmas present either of us could hope for. Everyone, on hearing the news, rushed up to the house to tell us how pleased they were for us. (Even the Stinsons unwound enough to ask us in for a drink.) So we had quite a gay lead-up to Christmas, instead of wondering how we were going to keep up a facade of jollity for the children's sake. We had a happy day, starting at six with the boys waking us all excitedly opening their stockings. I had given them a little cart and a rubber dinghy. The cart proved a Godsend as we could put all the beach things in it, and later taught Zulu to pull it, which he did very well, and sometimes with Rory in it as well. It was an awful slog up from the beach in the middle of the day once it had begun to be really hot, so it was a good investment.

Yvonne had visits from her cousin, David Fairbairn, who was in the South African army and stationed in Cape Town. It was his mother who she had lived with in Durban before joining us. We were also visited by John Wynn-Evans, a naval commander of a destroyer, who I had met at Anita's party. Yvonne went into the town to have a meal with David now and then, but we celebrated New Year together on our own, as neither of us felt like going to party. It had been quite a year, and we both wondered what the next one would bring. Little did we know, and it was just as well as it happened.

Mark had his sixth birthday 3 January, and we had a small party in the house and garden with the Myers, and Mummy and Charles brought Jane. Yvonne made some marvellous cakes, and we played games and all the children seemed to enjoy themselves.

1943

WE WERE HAVING SUPPER one night and Mummy and Charles were with us, and David Fairburn, when a South African called Marischel Murray arrived to call on Yvonne. He turned out to be an extremely nice little man who apparently knew some friends of hers who had suggested he looked her up. He asked if we would both go with him one evening to the 'little theatre'. He was interested in the arts, and this was a repertory company which he said was extremely good. We gathered he worked at the Censor's Office, and spoke several languages. We soon got to know him well, and I decided he must be a homo – although not obviously so. He was not in the LEAST interested in either of us from the sex angle. But he was kind, amusing, and very easy to get on with, and *just* the kind of male friend we needed. He lived in a flat in Seapoint in a wonderful position built right over the rocks. It was quite dramatic having dinner there, as the spray came right over the plate glass windows. He came to Bridget's christening in the little church in Camps Bay on 20 January. I was one of the Godmothers, and David a Godfather with a man called, Irvine a friend of Yvonne's, who came with his wife from Wynberg.

The boys got a craze on frog and tadpole hunting, and spent every possible moment at it. One of the doctor's sons, John Hawthorn, who Mark had a passion for, aided and abetted. He was much older, and knew exactly where to go to find the best specimens. His father was Irish and reputed to be very vague. Mummy had been advised to go instead to a Dr Lazarus, an up and coming young Jewish doctor who she found very good. Up to now we had not needed one, but he proved to be excellent when we did. Dr Hawthorn met me one day looking for frogs and tadpoles with the boys, and refused to believe I was their mother, and not their older sister!

Marischel suggested we called on a couple he knew, Iris and Ernest Jappe, who were living in a flat near our little beach. Ernest was invalided out of the South African army and had just missed going to Singapore. He and Iris were older than Yvonne and I, but had an adorable baby girl of Bridget's age. We got to like and know them quite well, and Iris joined us often on the beach. They also took us one day to the Rhodes Memorial, which is on a hill with wonderful views over both the Atlantic and the Indian Oceans. Ann Myers had been told by her husband that he now considered it safe enough for her to return to India, so I wondered if Betty might soon be on her way.

About this time I became worried about Yvonne. She kept complaining of very bad headaches and seemed very lethargic. I made her see Dr Lazarus who thought it all due to her period, which had not been regular since she left Singapore. He gave her injections which seemed to help a bit. Her aunt, Mrs Fairbairn, was down from Durban to see both her and David. Yvonne went in and had lunch with her once or twice, and also brought her back to see the children. Then one day, it was 8 February, we went into Cape Town together to shop. She was lunching with her aunt, and I going back to the children. She seemed particularly vague and did not seem to want me to leave her, but I had to get back for Bridget's lunch. About two-thirty a taxi arrived with a very distraught aunt rushing in to say Yvonne was very ill, and that the taxi driver was carrying her in as she was unable to walk. Luckily the boys were both at the Shorts, and Bridget asleep. So once we saw Yvonne comfortably on the bed – she was not unconscious, but had her eyes closed and she murmured her head was terrible – I rushed down to the Shorts' to telephone for Dr Lazarus. He came almost at once, and said he suspected meningitis. Apparently there was nothing we could do but keep an all-night watch. When Phyll brought the boys back I explained that Yvonne was very ill, and so they must be very quiet going to bed. I moved Bridget's cot into my room and, when they were all asleep, persuaded the aunt to have some supper while I sat with Yvonne. She was still conscious and kept murmuring, 'Oh my head, please try to do something for it.' I felt so useless in being unable to help her. When the aunt returned, I departed to bed with the understanding she would wake me in two hours to take over. It was well under that, when I woke to hear her saying in a near hysterical voice, 'Come quickly.' I ran into the room, and with one glance at the bed I was certain Yvonne was dead. The aunt refused to accept it, and kept wailing, 'It's not possible.' I tried to pacify her, and said I would go and phone for the doctor, at the same time waking Gertie so she had someone with her in the house, but only told Gertie that I had to get the doctor quickly.

I dressed and ran up the road to Phyll Short who was still up, and a great help. Dr Lazarus appeared almost as soon as I got back to the house, and confirmed what I already knew. To my relief he said he would call an ambulance as there would have to be a post-mortem. For the children's sake this was obviously the best thing, and I asked him to phone my mother at seven when I knew she would be awake. Mrs Fairbairn was horrified at the thought of Yvonne being moved, but Dr Lazarus insisted. She then asked me to go in and remove her wedding ring as she could not do it herself. I was so stunned by it all, that I did as she wanted. Then I realised the meaning of the phrase 'she had gone'. That exactly described it; she was no longer there. It was the first time I had ever seen anyone dead, but I felt cold and unemotional and as if it was all happening in a dream. The aunt was so worked-up and hysterical that the doctor gave her some sedatives, and I suggested she went and lay down on my bed; this she did once the ambulance and the doctor had arrived and departed.

I sat on the verandah watching the dawn come, and trying to realise what had happened and all the consequences. I thought of poor Dukie: as if life was not bad enough for him without him having this to bear as well. And poor Bridget with no mother or father. Mummy was up at the house by eight and a great comfort, so quiet and sensible in direct contrast to Mrs Fairbairn, who could not stop weeping, and I could tell thought it very odd of me not be showing some emotion. Poor thing, I felt very sorry for her as she was obviously genuinely fond of Yvonne, and felt responsible, being her nearest relative. Her sister was Yvonne's mother, but she was divorced and doing a war job in Ireland. David Fairbairn had been sent for, and came and fetched his mother and took her back to Cape Town. I told the boys that Yvonne had been taken off to hospital during the night, and took them all down to the beach as they were on holiday from school.

The result of the post-mortem came through and she had apparently died of cerebral haemorrhage, caused by a weakened artery. This was a rare condition, but one you are born with, and death always occurs before the age of thirty. She was twenty-nine. There was no means of diagnosing this before death, but accounted for her headaches and lethargy. A cousin of hers called Bar Barren, who had been out to visit us once or twice, turned up, and had a long talk with me about the situation.

He was a sensible young man, and was down in the Cape on leave from the Iranian oilfields where he worked. He was adamant that it was right that I should keep Bridget if I thought I could cope. With Betty Webber, hopefully, arriving in the not too distant future, and the fact that she had a baby girl the same age as Bridget, it seemed the obvious thing, but not according to the aunt who was directly opposed to the idea. I tried to point out both in letters and over the phone, that apart from the fact that I was the same generation as Yvonne, I was also Bridget's God-mother and wanted very much to keep her with us. Also, that I hoped our 'Nanny' with her daughter, who was born within a few days of Bridget in the same Singapore hospital, would soon be joining us, and therefore it would make an even 'family'. In the meantime I would try and get a South African or English girl as a Nanny to help me. She agreed to the latter idea, but I could not help feeling only because she would want someone herself if Bridget went to her.

She and David turned up ostensibly to see Bridget, but ended up with the aunt accusing me of using Yvonne's things, which I had no right to. The 'things' in question were a needle-case and a pair of scissors which happened to be in my work-basket. She told me that 'everything must be kept for Bridget to have when she was old enough'. I really saw red at this, and only just kept my temper. They departed, not giving any indication of what was to happen to all the clothes, etc. still in the wardrobe. I had thought I would give some to Amethe, and use the underclothes for myself. We were the same size and it was getting difficult to buy anything of this sort, also I knew Yvonne would have wanted me to have them. But I was so incensed at the insinuations that I was Pinching things.

A cable came from Mrs Hansen, Yvonne's mother, saying she thought it better if I could manage to keep Bridget, and then the aunt showed me one *she* had had saying, 'If you think it best to keep Bridget do so, but still feel she would be better with other children.' After this she told me she had engaged a Mrs Knight, a trained English Nanny, and she would be coming out to us in a few days' time. She turned out to be quite a nice woman and very efficient, but she seemed to expect a lot of time off. Anyway, the next thing I had was a letter from Mrs Fairbairn stating that Bridget and Mrs Knight were to go over to her at Wynberg for good the following week. No explanation, just the bald fact. I realised then that Mrs Knight had been in the know all the time, and had merely been sent over as 'sop' to me and for Bridget to get used to her. I discussed it all with Mummy and Charles, but it was obvious from the law that I had no leg to stand on. So in the end, poor Bridget, who we had all grown to love, was whisked away from us early one morning – 3 March to be exact – by David Fairbairn, who was sent to fetch her and Mrs Knight. I was so angry and upset at the way it had been done, and David was highly embarrassed when I asked *why* his mother had not come herself, murmuring something about her 'not being too well since the shock of Yvonne's death'. 'All the more reason for leaving Bridget here with *me*,' I retorted.

After they had departed, I went back into the house and had a good cry for the first time since she had died. I felt the whole thing was so wrong and selfish of the aunt, and could gladly have strangled her. The boys were so upset when they got back from school and found Bridget gone, as they had begun to regard her as their baby sister. Mummy and Charles were inclined to look at it from *my* point of view, as they felt keeping Bridget was going to be an extra responsibility on top of everything else. I was certainly much freer and enjoyed having the house to myself again, as I had not found Mrs Knight a very easy companion.

Mrs Fairbairn then wrote a letter saying she hoped I would understand that she was only acting for the best for everyone, and graciously suggested I kept any clothes of Yvonne's that would be of use to me. Having accused me of keeping things of hers that I had no right to, I did not feel inclined to have anything. I packed them all up and sent them, together with the sewing machine, by carrier over to the aunt. I heard nothing, although Anita, who lived in the same block of flats in Wynberg, said she had been presented with the machine, which she did not really want and knew had been so useful to me.

A few weeks later the whole lot was returned to me with a note from the aunt saying she really *did* want me to have them, and obviously it was because we were *both* upset that a misunderstanding had arisen and we had perhaps both acted hastily. As I presumed this was an apology for her original accusation, I decided I could only accept with what grace I could muster, and so wrote and thanked her. Before she went back to Durban she invited me over to have tea with her so I could see Bridget again. The boys were not asked, and I went on my own. Bridget seemed quite happy, but was very pleased to see me and wept when I left. I felt so terrible at having to leave her, as although she was too young to realise that Yvonne was not coming back, she had started to rely on me instead, and she was being let down twice in a short space of time.

ONE MORNING ON THE BEACH I was exercising Zulu before fetching the boys from school, and sat down on a rock next to a very tall, elderly, good-looking man whom I had not seen about before. We got talking, and he told me that he and his wife and daughter had just arrived out from England as he had been very ill with TB, and had been invalided out of the army – he was in the 12th Lancers – and told he must live abroad. He had been born on a sailing-ship entering Durban harbour, and lived in South Africa as a boy before being sent to school in England, and afterwards becoming a regular soldier. So South Africa was an obvious choice, and they had rented an old house up at the back near the boys' school. His daughter, Sarah, was nine, and she came over to join us after bathing in one of the pools, and soon afterwards his wife, another Virginia. They seemed very nice and asked me to take the boys to tea with them in a day or two. We soon became great friends, and although Sarah was three years older than Mark, she was very good with the boys, and they were used to Carmel and Edna.

I was beginning to get in touch with most of the friends I had lost in the general exit from Singapore. Pat Holden and her baby, Sally – I had taken the boys to her first birthday party just before we left – had got to Jamaica where her parents lived; but Pat had had no news of Peter, her husband, who was in the Sherwood Foresters, but seconded to the Malay Regiment. I also heard from Mary Brooke, who had helped me pack on my last night in Singapore. She had got safely back to England. Joan wrote that she had joined the Wrens. I also got a letter from Aunt Rose saying she and Uncle Arthur approved of the way I was trying to make a settled home for the boys, and then a marvellous one, of two closely written pages, from *him*. He told me not to worry too much about finances, and there was no reason why I should not live comfortably, and he knew he could trust me not to be extravagant. He also added that if I *was* short of cash, I was to draw on the firm in London and he would see it through. This took a great weight off my mind as, although I was managing on what I had, it was impossible to know how long the war would last and what expenses might occur. It was good to hear from him too: how life at Garroch was going on with a very reduced staff and many shortages. They had their two small grand-daughters, Charlotte and Georgina Paley, living there with their nurse, while their parents were both in Egypt. He seemed to think the war news was not *too* bad, and was optimistic about the firm's recovery after everything was over. 'We may have lost a few feathers,' he said, 'but there will still be a chicken when the end comes, though perhaps showing signs of moult and a little bedraggled.' I was much heartened by this, as a letter previously from his brother, Bertie, had been in a very different vein, indicating that I should economise even further, and generally very depressing. Afterwards I realised that this was because one was an optimistic, and the other the opposite. Also Bertie had lost his only son quite early on in the war.

We all seemed to have a bad bout of illness. My mother was by far the worse, with an agonizing carbuncle on the back of her neck. Then Mark kept running temperatures and having trouble at night with wet beds. I took him to a nice child specialist on Dr Lazarus' recommendation. He assured me there was nothing organically wrong, merely the shock of being parted from his father, etc. Then, on top of all this, I felt very ill myself and found I had a high temperature with my neck glands badly swollen. Dr Lazarus came and decided it was probably 'Tick Bite Fever' and suggested I had the injections, as it would take a week to get the result of a blood test. I said 'Yes' to that, as I hardly knew how I was going to cope with my mother ill as well, and no one but Gertie who was not all that bright. Of course I knew my friends would rally round, but they all had enough to do of their own. I told the boys that the doctor said I would die if I got out of bed, so I managed with that threat – if not a completely true one – to keep some control over them. Doff and Sven Barton kept them with them after school, and gave them their lunch.

Dr Lazarus made a bosh shot in his intravenous injection, which had to be done *three* times before eventually getting into the vein. The other two went into the skin in between, and my arm came up in a swelling as big as a golf ball. This was agony, so I got Gertie to go down to the chemist and ask him to ring the doctor for instructions. She came back after about an hour with some anti-flagistion which, when applied, gave me almost instant relief. Phyll, who had been in Cape Town and picked the boys up from Doff's was horrified when she heard my story. Zulu never left my side all this time, except to be let out in the garden to pee. Later, when we were all recovered, he went down to Mrs Northy's house and pinched her joint of meat off her kitchen table. She did not want to worry me, so I only heard about it later from Vernon. Meat was getting very scarce for all of us, and I could not possibly supply his 'pound of flesh' (a day).

Although it was meant to be Autumn, it had been hot for a long time now, and the garden was very dried-up – to keep any kind of lawn, it had to be watered morning and night. I talked to Mr Stinson on several occasions when we were both using our hoses, as there was only a low stone wall between the two gardens. He told me that his son had gone off to university, and that his wife had a bad back and was having to lie-up most of the time, mostly at the back of the house and in the sun. He asked me if I would rent him our garage where he wanted to keep a boat and a trailer, so I agreed to this. He then suggested I went in for a drink to discuss terms. I was somewhat surprised, as up to then had got the impression he thought I was what the South Africans called 'a high-hat English woman'. Anyway, he could not have been more friendly and talkative, wanting to discuss the war and world situation. Mrs Stinson appeared, apparently not too sick, and insisted on mixing our drinks, but not sitting down, or having one herself. I knew this was often the South African male attitude towards their wives, and felt acutely embarrassed by it. I left as soon as I could, and from then on was on very good terms, if fairly distant, with them both.

Mummy was fully recovered by her birthday, 16 July, and on

the same day I got news from Roper's mother that she had received a postcard from him saying he was well, but dated over a year ago. Still, it was the first definite news and we all rejoiced at it. The results of my blood test had come through, and apparently I had glandular, or tick, fever. I did feel awfully tired at times, so when I got an invitation from the Maydons, who had moved to Hermanus – a place on the coast about eighty miles from Cape Town – to go down and stay with them, I felt it might be a good thing to accept and get away for a bit. The Bartons had offered several times to have the boys who seemed keen on the idea, so I said 'yes'. The boys slept the night with them before I left, and when I went to see them, were so happily engrossed in something, that they hardly troubled to say goodbye. Charles ran Zulu and me into the town where Virginia had spent a couple of nights, and then she and I drove down to Heramus together. It seemed that winter had suddenly arrived, as it blew and rained most of the way and was even foggy on the pass. But it was hot and sunny by the time we arrived at their very attractive thatched-roofed house right on the sea. We were a little nervous at Conn's reaction to Zulu, as Virginia had not told him that we were bringing him, but his remark was typical with 'Oh, I see you have brought Fido.' Unfortunately 'Fido' disgraced himself the next day before breakfast by pinching the Sunday joint off the kitchen table. Poor David, their Basutoland house-boy and cook, was too terrified to do anything but yell and wring his hands. On hearing this, I guessed it might be something to do with Zulu, so ran to the scene of the crime and managed to wrench the joint out of his mouth. I handed it back to David, suggesting he cooked it and we would say nothing about it.

Virginia and Conn and I were sitting on the verandah drinking coffee after eating our lunch, when around the corner of the house came Zulu with the joint, though now considerably smaller, hanging from his jaws. I rushed to my feet, but he was faster than me and immediately clamped down and started to eat it. I could do anything with him except take a bone away. That would have been tempting providence, so I retreated with Virginia and Conn laughing uproariously, particularly when I confessed what had happened earlier. I found Conn very easy to get on with, and he was full of amusing stories. After leaving the army, he had become quite a famous big game hunter and had written the Lonsdale Library book on the subject. Most of his 'heads' had been given to the Norwich Museum. When he married Virginia ten years earlier, she was twenty-five and he fifty. Things had gone fine to start with, particularly with the birth of Sarah, but now he was desperately worried as he was able to do little, and Virginia was a very energetic person.

I found her a good companion, and we enjoyed doing the same things. We went for long walks up on the hills above Hermanus, with wonderful views of the coast for miles. It was quite a small town, not much larger than a village, but there were a lot of houses mostly scattered up the hills and along the coast, but there were also long stretches of scrub-land and beautiful deserted sandy beaches. The bathing was excellent for surfing, with waves coming in over quite shallow sand. The 'lagoon', which was situated eight miles north of the town, was a paradise for birds. An enchanting place with only a very few holiday shacks, looking like bird watchers' hides, along the shores. Mr Stinson had told me he owned one of these, and I thought how ideal it would be for a holiday with the children, but doubted if he would ever consider renting it. The time passed only too quickly, and we both had to get back as Virginia was fetching Sarah for her half-term from Herchel, her boarding school in Cape Town.

On returning, we found that Mummy and Charles had got the house ready as Gertie had disappeared, but there was very bad news as word had come through to Trudy that Jack had died the year before. She had apparently taken it very well, though nobody could bring themselves to tell Jane. My mother was marvellous, but obviously terribly upset; though she had tried to steel herself to the likelihood, the shock was still tremendous. Charles thought it would be a good idea if he took her away for a holiday, and they were planning to go to Stellanbosch, which was inland in the very pretty orchard country and where there was a good hotel.

The boys had seemed very pleased to have me back, but had got on very well with Doff and Sven. Virginia stayed for a few days with Sarah, and we took her to see a film called *Casablanca* with Ingrid Bergman and Humphrey Bogart which we thought marvellous, though a bit over Sarah's head. I had promised the boys, who had been left behind with Gertie – and asleep – that I would take them to *their* first film the following week. It was *Pinocchio* which they adored in parts, but were also terrified (especially Rory) by the witch.

I had a visit from a girl called Marjorie Hill, who was a sister of someone on the boat from India whom I had got to know. She had given Marjorie my address and so she appeared one afternoon, saying she had left her two little girls, Caroline and Mary-Clare, on the beach with their English nanny. I gather that she herself did a war job in the town, and her husband was a regular 'Sapper' in India. This was her day off. She was *so* nice and, by the time we had finished lunch, I felt I had known her for years. We took the boys down to the beach and joined up with the girls, who were so immaculately turned out in smocked dresses with sun-bonnets to match that we all secretly wondered how they would 'fit in'. The boys quickly disappeared to join their friends who were mucking about in the pools in their usual old clothes, and I could not help feeling rather sorry for the little girls who were obviously too much under the thumb of their nanny.

Gertie, who had been ill, finally told me she was leaving. I was not in the least surprised, and in some ways quite relieved. In the meantime I told Trudy I would house her 'nanny', who was about to go back to England, but wanted a temporary job before she left, and Trudy had already got someone to take her place. She was a nice girl, though inclined to want to 'discipline' the boys too much which they resented coming from a stranger. Still, it enabled me to go out occasionally, and it so happened at this time that I had been left a small legacy from an uncle. Joan had written and told me that it was meant to be divided between the three of us, but of course Jack's share would go to his children. The Jeppes, who had got hold of two good coloured sisters who wanted jobs, suggested that I had one and they had the other, and, in return, I asked them both to come out one night to celebrate my legacy. The were like a couple of children going to their first party, as they had been tied by the leg with their baby and no help up to then. I also asked Mummy and Charles, and Marischel Murray. We had dinner at the Café Royal and then went to a pretty bad show, and ended up at Marischel's for nightcaps on the way home. It had been fun, we decided, despite a bad start with Charles' car, which I had taken back home with the idea of taking the Jeppes and myself down to pick up Mummy and Charles. Nothing would induce it to start, and Ernest had had to go down to the garage for help. Still, we had got going in the end, then, to top it all, the next day I got a postcard from Roper. This had very odd phrasing to fit in with the 'Japanese Imperial Army card', which gave questions which were filled in by the sender. In this case, 'ALL IS – *well*', PLEASE SEE THAT – all is *taken care of*.' The postmark was Thailand, which was where we had already gathered they had been sent. If they were up in the hills the climate would be better than Malaya. My letters up to that stage had consisted of one page back and front, which I wrote on the Northy's typewriter in order to get more on it. Now we were suddenly informed that this was to be reduced to twenty-five *words* only, but two photos would be allowed and could be sent every fortnight. As I had a good Leica camera, I felt this to be quite a concession, but almost impossible to communicate in twenty-five words, although the photos, maybe, would give a better record of the boys and our surroundings.

I received a letter from Dukie's mother saying how sorry she and her husband were that I was not allowed to keep Bridget, which they had thought would have been far the best solution. She also said that they had had a postcard from Dukie saying that he was in Thailand, and she hoped (as I had written to her) that Roper received my letter informing them of Yvonne's death before the one I had also written to him. I had felt if Roper broke the news to him it would be so much better. As it turned out, that is what did happen.

The so-called winter – our summer – seemed to last a very short time, and then suddenly it was spring with masses of wild flowers growing everywhere up at the back of the house and along the shore. Arum lilies and tiny gladiolus in every imaginable colour. The proteas, large flowers with succulent foliage, were considered the most beautiful, but apart from their colour I thought them too coarse and much preferred some of the smaller varieties. The stream up behind the house was as clear, and clean as crystal, and we often went there for picnics.

My mother and I spent three mornings a week helping to cut sheepskin for the RAF. She also worked in the Red Cross restaurant kitchen, which was run in aid of POWs. There was heaps of voluntary work, but I could not do much until Betty arrived, and she was hoping to get to us by Christmas, depending on her getting a berth.

Doff thought that Mark had grown out of their school and at six could go to the local one, so he started there and seemed to have settled down quite well. He walked there on his own as it was only just at the bottom of the hill. I gathered he spent a lot of time looking out of the window at the sea, and showed little interest in reading. I tried to help him at weekends, and at bedtime, but then he always thought *I* should read to *him.*

One of the wives from Malaya who had made her way to Cape Town was Grace Andrea. Her husband had been in command of the Malay Regiment, and although we had not known them very well, she got in touch with me, and she had two sons about the same age as Mark and Rory. She was living in a bungalow in the grounds of the Bishop's Palace, as the bishop was her uncle. We went and spent a day with them there, and we all enjoyed ourselves; the boys trying to ride bikes, which I could not let them have safely at Camps Bay, and mucking about in a stream at the bottom of the garden while Grace and I talked. Another very nice woman, who was a friend of Grace's, was Ursula Hamilton-Moore. She was living out at St James on the other coast, but came into Cape Town daily to do a war job as her two daughters were both at school all day. Ursula's husband had been a planter but also a volunteer, and she had heard that he too was in Thailand. She was a particularly sweet, good-natured person, so ready to sympathise with one's troubles while making light of her own. I got to know her well and we often lunched together. She had a serenity and inner radiance which seemed to shine out of her eyes, and was so *definite* in her belief that all would come right in the end for us. She had known Yvonne quite well, and was very upset at her death, and felt that without doubt, Bridget should have stayed with me.

I saw Virginia Maydon quite often, and she suggested that we all went to Hermanus for Christmas. They were living in a different house, some miles from the town and near the Rivera

Hotel, which was situated on the coast with a beautiful sandy beach about halfway between Hermanus and the lagoon. It got very booked up, so she advised me to get rooms some time before, and I hopefully got an extra one for Betty and Valerie. I could hardly believe it when I got back from Cape Town one afternoon and found them both already installed in the house. They were not allowed to give us any warning of their arrival, but had managed to get a taxi out to my mother's who had taken them both up to the house. The boys were so thrilled to see Betty again, and Valerie, who was the same age as Bridget, and seemed a very friendly and easy child. Betty and I had so much to catch up with, we stayed up half the night talking. She had had no word of Peter and so, of course, feared the worst. Apparently quite a lot of the 'Gunners' had been sent up to China from Singapore. It was wonderful to have her there, so reliable and good with the children, I felt a new woman. We soon got into a routine, but I did not think it worth while starting a permanent job before the New Year. Sadly, Phyll and Diana Short were about to go back to the Persian Gulf, but Quinny was to be left behind in boarding school. I was going to take on her maid, Lena, who seemed a nice girl and, although not up to Virginia's standard, infinitely better than Gertie. (The Jeppes' maid's sister never materialised.) It was decided she would have a holiday, and come to us when we got back on the 27 December. I would have to put Zulu into kennels, but the people who I had got him from agreed to have him. Mr Stinson told us to go and visit them at their lagoon house and he would take the boys out in his boat. His wife was still 'suffering' with her back and so they were spending a month there so she could do nothing but lie in the sun.

Early in December – now high summer – we set forth in Charles's car which he had lent us for our stay in Hermanus, as he and Mummy had decided to stay 'put' over Christmas, but would be with Trudy and Jane, and the baby, John, for the day. We got to Hermanus in time for lunch and found we had a good room overlooking the sea, but there had been a muddle over Betty and Valerie and for the first few days they had to move until finally they got next door to ours. We saw the Maydons every day, and their house was up a road opposite the hotel. Sarah had a school friend staying, but they were both good at coping with the boys and Valerie. The beach in front of the hotel was not good for surfing, so for this we went along to one called the Fille-klip beach which was small, but had ideal short surf; very easy for beginners, but the waves too big for Valerie's age and, because she was not afraid of them, she kept going out too far and being knocked down. Virginia introduced us to a Ruth Van Tonder, who was staying in the hotel with her daughter, Olga, about Sarah's age. She seemed very nice and friendly, and so was her husband, George, who appeared a few days later. He was fat and jolly, and bald, and they ended up being my first, and very good, Afrikaner friends. I quite often had a drink with them, and they told me they had more friends coming and I must join them whenever I wanted to. George worked in a 'Trust Company' in Cape Town, and looked after all Conn Maydon's affairs.

We had our Christmas lunch with the Maydons. Virginia was marvellous, but Conn was in a very queer mood and he ended up leaving the dining-table before we had finished, muttering that he could not take so many children and the noise they made. Virginia told us not to worry, and afterwards surprised us all by playing and singing to an accordion, on which she was very accomplished, though I had not known about it before. All the children joined in, and then we played games in the garden. The following night I joined the Van Tonders in a pretty wild party with their friends and various others, which lasted until the early hours. I found the South African men very nice on their own, but rowdy and difficult in a party, and inclined to try and take advantage of a 'lone' girl like myself. George was never like this, and was amused when his 'Boss', who was one of the party, told him the next day that he considered me 'a cold, hard, calculating English woman'. We laughed over this verdict, and I said I thought it was not a bad image, as long as my real friends saw through it.

We said goodbye to the Maydons, and started off back home the following day. We found Mummy and Charles had got everything ready for us, but not unexpectedly, Lena had failed to turn up. We had a quiet New Year's Eve with Mummy and Charles, and so ended 1943.

WE SETTLED DOWN TO OUR NORMAL ROUTINE, with Zulu none the worse for his time in kennels. Betty and I wished so much that Bridget was with us as a companion for Valerie, although Rory got very attached to her and played with her by the hour, particularly when he came home from school before Mark.

I had read in the paper that help was needed by anyone who could use a paint brush, and on applying I gathered this was in preparation for a very ambitious 'Liberty Cavalcade' which was to be held for a week on a large bit of waste land near Seapoint, organised by the combined services and our allies. The preliminary work was to start in the top-storey of a garage in the town, where we would paint the scenery, etc, needed. I thought it sounded interesting, so presented myself for the job and was accepted by a Mrs Voss, who was in charge. She seemed

Valerie Webber (Betty's daughter) and Rory at Camps Bay

very easy to get on with, and had quite a fascinating 'arty' appearance. I was slightly taken aback when the next day I was immediately given strips of 'tartan' which had to be enlarged to two feet high by six feet; these to be used for the fronts of the stalls in the Scottish section. It had to be done to scale of course, and I was more than unnerved when a Brigadier from a Scottish regiment came and watched me at work, finally moving off without comment. The other girls working there, many young marrieds like myself, proved to be very friendly and we had a very amusing and interesting three months.

Virginia Maydon had taken over the Jeppes' flat for when she had to be in Cape Town, as they had moved to Wynberg. So I was relieved to find her there one afternoon when, after getting off the bus, I read a news placard saying 'Atrocities committed by the Japs on their POWs'. Not that there was anything one could do, but it was a comfort to talk to a friend. She was not feeling too good as she was worried about Conn, who had not been really well since Christmas – part of the reason for his outburst – and she herself had to go into hospital for an operation. Conn was at his club, so I saw him most days and got up to see Virginia whenever I had the car. I had Sarah for the weekend, and after taking her back to school on the Sunday night I had dinner with Conn, as he wanted me to meet some people he knew called MacDougall who came from Norfolk, but were out there for the same reason as Conn, and apparently Herbert MacDougall had been very ill and was much older than Cicely. They seemed very nice and asked us out to their house near Wynberg, as they had one son, Quinton, with them who was about the same age as Mark, and another much older at school in England. I gathered that Cicely MacDougall soon hoped to go home as she said her husband's health had improved so much, and they wanted to get back to their other son and their house and estate – Cawston Manor in Norfolk. Later on when we visited them, they were packed up and ready to go, but told me to be sure to get in touch with them when we got home. I had said that I felt Roper would like to have a few months in Norfolk when he was first released, as he had been brought up there and was very fond of the country. Cicely said they might well have a house at Cawston that we could rent. It seemed a pipe-dream then, but one that did come about.

Rory's 5th Birthday with Author and Mark

Rory had his fifth birthday on 13 February with fourteen children to tea. Marischel Murray turned up with a girl photographer who took some enchanting candid photos of the children, and one in particular of Rory, covered with freckles, which later was published in a book she produced.

One morning I woke about four o'clock in the morning hearing noises outside my bedroom, and on looking out found Mr Stinson hosing down the roof. When I asked him what on earth was going on, he replied that the mountain was on fire and that he was taking precautions, as it would be dangerous to us both if it crossed the barrier of the road that went past the house and up round to Kloof-Nak. I pulled on some clothes and went outside, and it was a pretty awesome sight with the whole sky lit up. It was dawn before the fire brigade, who were out in strength, got it under control and we were able to retire to our beds. The children had slept through all the noise and clamour, but I had told Betty what was going on as she, of course, had woken.

Betty and Amathe Northy, now fifteen, became great friends and often went out together in the evening, which helped the monotony for them both. I had made friends with a girl called Mardy Gearing, who was a very good artist but 'helping out' at the studio-cum-garage for the Cavalcade. Things were hotting up there, and we were told that there would be at least three weeks' work down on the site before it opened, and were we both prepared to risk our necks on ladders and scaffolding? We said we were, but wondered what was in store. Mardy was engaged to a South African Marine who was in England, but whom she hoped to marry on his next leave home.

We finally got out to the site and found ourselves asked to do some fairly perilous work on some of the buildings, but also had to paint larger-than-life replicas of Greek guards for the entrance to their pavilion. We got our photos taken by the press doing this, and it appeared in the *Cape Times.* I had been asked if I would work in the English section during the week. This was to consist of a replica of an old English Inn, to be called 'Drake's Drum'. The 'serving wenches' were to be dressed in mob caps and long dresses with aprons, and the hours were to be from twelve noon to 2.00 p.m. and again from 6.00 p.m. to 9.00 p.m. 'Drake's Drum' was more or less finished and complete with very realistic looking 'oak beams' inside and out, sawdust floors and barrels to sit on, but by the night before the opening they were still without a 'stone' bridge which led over a stream to the Inn. At least the bridge was built, but with white cardboard sides waiting to be converted into 'stone'. Rather quaking inwardly, I undertook to do the job and found myself still quite late at night under arc-lights – though well protected by Zulu – desperately trying to finish. What appeared to be all the armed servicemen drove by in lorries – 'Drake's Drum' was situated at the entrance – and gave me the usual catcalls and whistles. Zulu growled and lay closer at all this, so I was not much worried.

Once open, everyone came to visit us, and Mummy and

Charles brought the boys on several occasions. They were, of course, much more impressed by all the marvellous tanks and and aeroplanes on display which they were allowed to climb in and out of. But for most people the Inn was a terrific success, and we were run off our feet. I found it quite difficult to keep a large order for drinks in my head if someone then waylaid me with another order. But everyone entered into the spirit of the thing and didn't get too annoyed if you made mistakes. George Van Tonder appeared one evening on his own, as Ruth was pregnant and feeling unable to move. He took me, after I had finished, to the American section, which consisted of a 'Western type' bar called the 'Dead Horse Gulch', which also had a dance floor with a marvellous negro band as well as a first-class cabaret. We had great fun and George, like so many fat men, was a very good dancer. It all seemed to end rather suddenly, and the Shiels, the couple who were running 'Drake's Drum', and the rest of us had a tearful farewell after the last night. We had been living in a make-believe world, and it was hard to realise we were coming down to earth. Still, the amount of money realised was quite considerable and, apart from that, it had given people a chance for a short time to forget the grimness of the rest of the world.

I was not too happy about Mark's school, and Doff Barton was thinking of closing her kindergarten as she was expecting a baby. So when I heard of a marvellous sounding private school over at Wynberg run by a Mrs Hood, who had a remarkable reputation for getting children interested in the three Rs, I decided to go over and see her. She had a wonderful personality, full of vitality and obviously dedicated to her job. We got on very well, and I explained our position. She was particularly interested to hear that Betty had Froebel training, and immediately asked if she would take on a job at the school. We had anticipated this, and discussed the idea. Betty was quite keen, and felt she would be better occupied that way, also Valerie would have other children of her own age. Of course it all depended on our getting somewhere else to live near the school. George's firm dealt in property among other things, and so I asked him to let me know if he heard of anything likely. I could have rented quite a nice little house in Wynberg, but it was very suburban and in a road among masses of others. Not at all what I wanted for myself and the children.

George came up with a perfect sounding farm-house at a place called Bergvliet in the Tokai Valley. This was only a mile from 'Deep River', a station on the main line from Cape Town to Simonstown, and only two stops on from Wynberg. We went to look at it: a very nice house and I was thrilled at the position and surrounding country, so I was terribly disappointed when George rang me up in a fury to say that the owner, without a word to him, had let it to some naval people called Ouvry.

George and Ruth came out the following week and drove me round the district, but without anything specific to look at. We went to the next door farm, which was called Bergvliet, belonging to an old couple called Jeffcott who George had met. On the road leading to the house, which was a beautiful example of the old Dutch farmhouse with white-washed walls and thatched roof, I spied what looked like two empty cottages set back in the fir woods that lined the road. George and Ruth, while saying I was mad, agreed to go and ask the farm manager about them. We found him at his very nice house situated near the farm buildings. His name was Nightingale, and he proved quite sympathetic, though obviously somewhat surprised, explaining that although the cottages had never been occupied and had been built for farm workers, they were rather primitive and hardly suitable. Still, I persuaded him to take us over them, and immediately saw there were great potentialities.

Each cottage consisted of two rooms, kitchen and a verandah – or stoep – in the front, running the whole length of the two. I suggested that it would be quite easy to knock a door through so the two main rooms connected, and turn one of the kitchens into a bathroom. The four outside lavatories were situated opposite the back doors from the kitchens. I was so enthusiastic that Nightingale agreed to consult with the Jeffcotts, and I suggested that if they agreed, I would pay for the bath and basin which would have to be installed, if they could do the job of knocking through and putting in a door.

I went home to tell the children and Betty who, unlike everyone else, was very keen on the idea, and the boys were thrilled at the thought of living on a farm. Mark had suddenly become 'farm conscious' and got a toy one that I had acquired second-hand from the MacDougals when they left. I was in some suspense until I heard from George that the Jeffcotts were quite willing – and to foot the bill – but would like to meet me before making a final decision. He took me out there, and they were both very sweet and understanding. Mr Jeffcott was older than her and not at all well, so she did most of the talking. They had two sons and a son-in-law all in the South African army, so were most sympathetic when they learnt that Roper was a POW, and fully understood why I wanted to live out in the country, as it was what they liked themselves. But she *did* see the cottages were very primitive with no light or sanitation. I explained that I was used to this from my Malayan days, and thought we could easily cope with that side. Betty, too, had been brought up in India as a girl, so the thought of living without mod-cons held no horrors for her either. So it was agreed, and the work was to start at once. We went with Nightingale to have another look round, and he explained that the water tank on the roof was controlled from the farm so, when the cowman was cleaning out his sheds, the supply would be cut off. There was apparently no means of telling when the tank was full, except when it overflowed onto the roof. This was fairly primitive, and would mean that when we had the geyser on – run on wood – it was possible for the water to cease running and the geyser blow up unless the fire was immediately put out. This, we found, was quite a major snag when we eventually moved in, especially when one was about to bath three extremely dirty children.

I took my mother and Charles out to see it, and they thought it was a marvellous place for the children, though obviously they were sad about our leaving Camps Bay, but agreed with my main reason for moving for them to attend the 'Little People's School'. This was all arranged, and Betty would take all three to Wynberg each morning on the train. The school was very close to the station at Deep River. I would drive them to, and fetch them from, 'Deep River', unless I was going or coming from Cape Town, when I would take them by car. A jolly, fat woman, whose husband worked on the farm, agreed to come in each morning. Her name was Katie, and I felt with her there to do the housework, I would be free to buy the food and probably do a half-day job in Cape Town once we got settled. I bought a second-hand Austin Ten and thought, if I did get a job, that Zulu could be left sitting in it quite happily. The Red Cross restaurant did not mind my taking him in there, and leaving him in the ladies' cloakroom. The Bartons all came out to look at 'The White Cottage', as I named it, and were enchanted with the place and the surroundings, and fully supported me in what most people seemed to consider my wild plans.

We went out to Bergvliet several times for picnics and week-ends, and were joined there one day by the Andreas, who were equally enamoured with the place. We cooked sausages on a wood fire, and the children all had rides on a farm cart that was out collecting firewood. The men working on the farm seemed very friendly, and most of them had worked there and for the Jeffcott family for generations. They were all negroes from 'up country', as opposed to the Cape coloured, and therefore had the reputation of being much more reliable and trustworthy, and hence, Mr Nightingale said, he had practically no labour trouble. The nearest coast was at Muizenberg under twenty minutes away, so we felt we would have the best of both worlds, especially as the sea on the Indian Ocean was much warmer than at Camps Bay, which was on the Atlantic.

We planned to move in time for the children to start at the new school by the next term; so they would be on holiday anyway for Easter. Then they all got whooping cough in turn. Mark, who never seemed very ill with contagious diseases, was over it by the time we eventually moved, but both Rory and Valerie were quite ill and went on being sick with it for a long time. Still, the actual move had gone well, helped by both Mummy and Charles, and Marischel who was marvellous at bringing out car-loads of stuff. I bought some rather nice white oak furniture made by a craftsman in Cape Town: a long sideboard-cum-book-case and a desk. The sitting-room was tiny, but I put a divan in there as a sofa, and two beds in my bedroom so we could have Virginia and Sarah to stay. Betty and Valerie shared a room, and the boys. Theirs was larger and so doubled up as a playroom, but they mostly used the long verandah. The bathroom had turned out quite well, despite the rather Heath Robinson arrange-ments. I rather enjoyed lying in the bath feeding the wood geyser with fir-cones thrown from a sitting position, into the little oven that heated the water. A lot landed in the bath, but as long as the fire was kept going the water remained very hot. We did have some rather frantic moments when, having made a good fire, the water would abruptly stop and there was nothing for it but to pour water into the oven, but this happened quite rarely.

It had been rather wet, but suddenly became hot and sunny and so we were able to be outside most of the day, and the children began to pick up. It was the best possible spring-like weather, and all the grass under the trees was fresh and green. Katie was so slow she drove us mad, but kind and helpful. She usually brought her youngest child with her, but she was a nice little girl and played with Valerie, who was not able to keep up with the boys as they spent most of their time with the men on the farm. Everyone seemed very good natured about them. It was mainly a dairy farm and Mark's ambition was to accompany the milk carts which, drawn by horses, did a long round starting at 4.00 a.m. I told him maybe he would be allowed to go later on in the summer, when the early mornings would be warmer. Betty seemed to settle down well, and was perfectly happy being left with Zulu as 'protector' if I went over to see my mother,

Mark, Valerie and Rory at Bergvliet Farm, Tokai Valley

or do some shopping. Mrs Hodd agreed it would be better if all the children started together, and she could manage without Betty until the two youngest had completely recovered, so they had extra long holidays. There was quite a lot going on, as the earth road that led to the farm also went on to various small-holdings, mostly native owned, so there were numerous donkeys and pony carts, but no cars; and there was also a riding school further up the valley. Marjorie Hill appeared one day riding with a friend called Cecilia Caldicott whom I had met before in Cape Town. She told me that she had been in love with Noel Roper-Caldbeck, whom she knew in India before she was married. She now had three boys, and her husband was still in the Indian Army. After that she often appeared on her own, as she kept a horse up at the riding school. Much to the children's delight, she rode right up to my bedroom window where I was recovering from a go of bronchitis, and carried on a long conversation without getting off the horse. Mrs Jeffcott also came to see me, bringing a large bunch of flowers from her garden. She came in and sat down, and I thought her an exceptionally nice woman. She told me her husband was not at all well; he was in his late seventies, so worried about the farm with both sons away, and now Mr Nightingale was ill, and might have to have an operation.

Mummy and Charles came over to see me, and we all sat on the verandah in the lovely sunshine. I was feeling a bit weak still, but when Mark came back with our letters, which were delivered to the Jeffcotts, he had a postcard from Roper which, to my joy, mentioned Zulu, which obviously was his only means of indicating that he had received some of my letters, so it was marvellous that we had established contact, despite all the restrictions. I felt so terribly sorry for Betty who still had heard nothing of Peter. She never showed any resentment, but I knew it must be very difficult for her not to give way to her feelings sometimes, especially when I had been lucky enough to have had news on three occasions. Mrs Jeffcott mentioned that her sixteen year-old grand-daughter was coming to stay, and wondered if Betty would like to go to the ballet with her while she was there. Betty was only too delighted, and we both felt we would like to help Mrs Jeffcott in any way, as she herself would not leave her husband.

They had a good evening out, and did it in style as they went in the Jeffcotts' chauffeur-driven car.

The two younger children were not quite right and still whooping, so we decided that Betty would take Mark to the school and leave the others with me for a while longer. We drove them to the station and then spent the rest of the day playing about the place, or taking Zulu for walks. He horrified me by attacking first a goat and, on another occasion, a pig. These both belonged to native smallholdings, but neither were really damaged by the time I got him away, and the owners were quite good tempered about it. Still, I was worried after the other episode at Camps Bay, and despite the Jeffcotts' 'protection' I felt it might lead to trouble. I bought him a muzzle, a fairly easy one which enabled him to open his mouth but not wide enough to get a grip of anything. Betty and Mark were both full of the 'Little People's School', and seemed to like it there so much that the other two could not wait to go too – we often walked up to the lake behind the cottage. It was quite large and very attractive, with a lot of wild swans and ducks, but a great colony of egrets nested high up in the big old trees that surrounded two sides of the lake. During the nesting season, which was getting into full swing, their droppings killed all the grass below, and made the most ghastly smell. To add to all this, there were hundreds of small baby birds lying in the shambles under the trees; either pushed or fallen from the nests. On the whole they were too young to feed themselves and the parent birds ignored them, so they just died of hunger. We stopped going there after a time, as we could not stand the carnage. Mrs Jeffcott told us this happened every year, but when the young they *had* managed to bring up were old enough, they migrated, returning the following spring.

After a few weeks Betty started to take all three with her to school, and the younger two seemed to like it as much as Mark. I went into Cape Town three or four days each week and met my mother at the Red Cross restaurant, where we both helped in the kitchens. The Ouvry family, who were installed in the original farmhouse I had hoped to rent, consisted of themselves and two children, a boy and girl about ten and nine years old. Captain Ouvry was stationed at Simonstown, where he took Jeremy off every day to a naval school. He was an odd man, I thought, and very thoughtless in many ways. They all rode, and had their own ponies, and he seemed to think nothing of arriving at the cottage, riding right over my pathetic attempts at creating a garden, and usually bringing his dog, Barney – a Dobermann Pinscher. Zulu did not approve of this, especially having his domain penetrated. One day they 'set to' and decided to fight it out. While I dashed for pepper, Captain Ouvry firmly sat on his horse shouting instructions. When the pepper had no effect, I grabbed one of the boys' cricket bats lying about, and brought it down on their noses, aiming rather more at his dog than mine. It did the trick, and I grabbed Zulu while Barney's master rode off whistling his dog and muttering something about my 'blasted dog', which I thought a bit cool as I had not invited him to visit me. I also was amazed that he never once got off his horse to help. Still, we got over this, and I was invited to dinner with them one night. Susan Ouvry said if I wanted to walk – our houses were about half a mile apart – it would be all right to bring Zulu as a chaperon, as Barney was shut up at night. It was still light when I arrived, but after dinner, about ten-thirty, when I said I must leave, it was pitch black and I did expect Arthur Ouvry to offer to see me home. But no such suggestion came, and he casually stated, 'You'll be all right with that dog of yours.' I was not too happy, as being a Saturday night the farm men were inclined to have a few too many drinks and get a bit wild, singing and dancing somewhere among the trees, although they never came close to our cottage. I heard their voices and drum-beat as I got near, and then one of the men, seeing a figure approach, raised a stick and shouted at me. I knew he had not recognised me, so hopefully called out, 'Put that stick down you madman, it's only me.' There was a slight embarrassed pause, then they all laughed and made jokes; so with some relief I got by, but was not sorry to reach the cottage.

I bought some australope chickens and a rabbit for the children, and made an attempt at a kitchen garden, getting one of the farm men to come and dig a patch at the side of the house. I put up a low fence of wire netting thinking it would keep out most marauders, but just when my row of carrots, lettuces, etc. were beginning satisfactorily to show themselves, I woke one night to an odd sound which I could not define. Grabbing a torch and a coat, I went out to find six of the farm horses trampling about on my precious vegetable patch. I shooed them off, but nearly wept the next morning when I surveyed the scene of devastation. So much for the vegetables, though we did start all over again, and I was determined to grow some kind of hedge in the front to keep my 'horsey' friends out. This was fairly ambitious, as the quickest growing hedge takes quite a time to get established, even in that climate. However, I was told that if I wanted to ensure fast growth, far the best method was to use human urine. So every morning I duly emptied the three children's 'potties' over the pathetic little sticks of box. I was caught in the act by Marjorie Hill, who rode up one morning with a Princess Radizwell. They could not stop laughing when they realised what I was up to, though neither of them paid the slightest regard for my so-called barrier.

My mother was worried about Charles, who seemed very unsettled and really wanted to go and live in England. Now the war news was so much better, Joan had written to say that if they did decide to come home, she had heard that a cousin of my mother's, who lived in Selsey near Chichester, would be willing to let them have her house as she was helping her daughter with her young children while the son-in-law was away. Mummy did not want to leave us behind, and I thought it was stupid for us to move again, now we were settled at Bergvliet and all the children happy at school. Also it would be wrong to take children to England before the war, anyway in Europe, was over. We discussed all this at some length and I managed to persuade her in the end that we would be perfectly all right, and had a lot of friends nearby which made all the difference. Also the Jeffcotts were so kind and helpful in every way, that it was not as if we were completely on our own. They had found out that there was a ship sailing in a month's time, and that there was a chance they might be able to get a berth in her, and with any luck we would be following them the next year. So the next time we met it had all been arranged, and I knew they were both relieved.

The weather was really hot, and all the grass under the trees disappeared and became very dusty, but I enjoyed the days I had on my own with Zulu, although lots of different people turned up unexpectedly as we had no phone. Wendy Grant was one of them. She had been in Singapore, and both Roper and I had known her husband, John, long before they were married. She was living with her two small boys, Ian and Peter, out on the coast at St James's where Ursula was, and she had told her where we were. I was delighted to see her; she asked us to visit them any weekend, and the bathing was good there and Ian the same age as Mark. We often went to the sea, although Muisenberg got very crowded at the weekends; we sometimes took our tea there after school. There were miles of marvellous deserted sand and the waves quite gentle as there was no wind, so the children could run about safely on their own. Betty felt that Valerie, being younger, got rather tired after school, so I usually took the boys on their own.

Mummy and Charles came out to see the children just before they left, and I spent their last night with them at a hotel in Cape Town. Marischel, as usual, turned up trumps and took us out to dinner at the Café Royal, and as Mummy was dead against my seeing them off, the Van Tonders had offered to take me out for the day to Golduna Bay where there are masses of wild flowers for a short period. I felt dreadful saying goodbye that night, but it seemed better that way, as I was starting early and they had not to be on board until midday. Anyway, Marischel was taking them to the docks and would see them safely settled, as he was allowed in on a pass because of his job. Altogether it seemed the best solution, and Charles was obviously much happier at their decision to leave. He had very much lacked male company, and was looking forward to seeing his brothers again. Mummy would be able to see something of Joan too, as she was stationed at Portsmouth, which was not too far away. I had a very good day with Ruth and George, and they took me all the way home. Betty and the children had managed all right in my absence, as the Jeffcotts had got their chauffeur chap to take them to the station, and fetch them in the evening.

The next day proved rather a disaster. I had a bad back for no particular reason, then, after leaving the children, I was attacked by Katie who said I had accused her of stealing, merely because I had asked her if she had seen something I could not find. Then, on top of all that, Zulu, whose muzzle I had failed to put on, actually killed a goat. We were out for a walk, and he had gone quite a long way ahead of me out of sight round a bend, when I came on this awful scene with him standing over his victim, quite a small animal, but according to the owner a very valuable one. A crowd collected and, feeling a bit sick, I told the man to come and see me the next day and I would pay him for it, and made a retreat.

Then, on meeting Betty, she said she was suffering from a migraine and had to go straight to bed. I had a bad night worrying about Zulu, and wondering, if he became too much of a nuisance, whether I had better not be sensible and try and get him a good home elsewhere. I hated the idea as we all loved him, and he was such a good companion and protector, if only he had not got this loathing for goats. A few days later Mr Nightingale, who had apparently recovered but did not look too well, came to see me, having heard the story about the goat. Mr Jeffcott and he were apparently now worried that he might start attacking the calves on the farm. I protested that this was very unlikely, as he never so much as glanced at them and never left me to go out hunting on his own. Nevertheless, he was obviously very worried about the situation, and I could only say that I would think about it. He indicated that if I did not get rid of Zulu, that the only alternative was for us to move.

Everything always seemed to go wrong at once, and the next thing that happened was that I got a summons to appear in Court, or £3 'admission of guilt'. I had been stopped by a policeman on my way through Wynberg, taking everyone to school, and asked why my licence was not on the windscreen. Rory had pulled it off and I had put it in the car pocket, intending to stick it on again the moment I got the chance. I produced it and showed it to the policeman, who muttered something under his breath but let me go. So now this. I was furious, as I knew the local South African police were automatically anti if you spoke with an English accent; also, that they got promotion by the number of convictions they produced. I decided, though inwardly quaking, that I must fight it out, so wrote to say I would appear in Court on such-and-such a date. The policeman was in the dock, and when asked by the magistrate if I had produced the said licence, he answered, no, I had not. This was too much, so I let out a gasp and when asked if I agreed with the statement, I gave an emphatic 'No', to which the magistrate smiled and asked why? I told him that I *had* shown the licence to the policeman, and explained that my small boy had only just pulled it off, and that I did not think it a good time, in the middle of the town, to stop and try and put it back. So he dismissed the case, much to my relief.

Mardie Gearing, who I had painted with at the Cavalcade, wrote to say she was getting married to Wilson Van de Byll quite soon, as he was getting unexpected home leave. She wanted me to go to the wedding and mentioned that I might like to go with Connie Whitley, whom we had both got to know during that time, and who had remained a friend whom I often met in Cape Town. I arranged to pick her up at Green Market Square, so we could go to the church together, but for some reason she did not turn up, so I decided to go on without her. As I left the Square, to my horror, the horn stuck on. Everyone in the vicinity stopped dead in their tracks and stared at me. I drew in to the side, but as I was dressed for a wedding, even down to the long white gloves, I did not feel inclined to open the bonnet, so looked round wildly for help. Two young men rushed up and soon stopped the ghastly noise by seizing some wires and pulling them apart. I could not have been more grateful to them, but was not able to do more than thank them profusely and rush off to the church; although late, I still thankfully got there before Mardie, who soon arrived looking really gorgeous. She was tall and good looking, and so was Wilson, so they made an attractive pair. I met several of our 'co-workers' at the reception at Kelvin Grove Club, and Connie also turned up there, explaining that her mother was late in arriving to look after her little girl.

Zulu had been sitting in the car all the time, as I could not shut him in the house; if I did, Katie refused to go in. She did most of our washing as well as the housework, but often turned up at odd times of the day according to the situation in her own house. Our cooking arrangements consisted of an antiquated oil stove. If the wicks were not trimmed very regularly, it quite often smoked so badly you could not see across the kitchen, and the soot and mess were indescribable. Despite all the snags, we loved living there and preferred it to Camps Bay. I was shown how to fix up a meat-safe-cum-ice-chest outside on the north side of the house. This stood on an old table inside a galvanised tin bath filled with water. By putting a sack over the safe, which was raised on bricks, and trailing the ends in the water, we kept our food and butter, etc. almost ice cold. It was a bore always having to trail over to the loos at the back, but at least there were four of them, and a dear old man came every day and cleaned them out. So many people, including Mrs Jeffcott, seemed amazed that we could stand such a life having been used to 'better things', but the climate certainly helped, and I think both Betty and I had the 'pioneer spirit' and rather enjoyed the challenge.

Mark gave Betty and me a fright one night when Betty discovered he was not in his bed at 4.00 a.m. It was moonlight, so I went over to the farm buildings, only to be met by one of the early milkers and led to a horse's stall, and there, literally underneath his feet, was Mark curled up and fast asleep. I led him back and he explained he had only just got up to look at his favourite horse, but an owl had shrieked and frightened him, so he had decided to stay where he was and must have gone to sleep. Soon after this I let him go on the milk round. This was his dearest wish, starting at 5.00 a.m. and returning around 11.00 a.m. All the way to Rhonderbosch and back – something he never forgot.

Susan Ouvry asked me to go to the Wynberg clinic with her twice a week and, as I now only did two mornings at the Red Cross, I told her I would. Most of the patients were black women. My job was to help them fill up a form for contraceptives. I could not help being amused at the different reactions to the question 'how many needed a week?' Some were quite indignant about this and replied 'seven, of course', and another, with a smirk, 'fourteen' – night and day, I thought.

One weekend the Andreas and the Caldicotts all came out for a picnic, seven boys and Valerie; not that she minded, and they were all very nice to her on the whole, but still I thought of Bridget, and wondered how she was getting on, as I never heard. We cooked sausages and chops outside, and afterwards they all played wild games in the woods. Rory was very indignant at being grabbed by Cecilia before lunch to try and wash off some of the dirt, including his huge freckles. They really got filthy as it was so dusty. Marjorie Hill and I often took Zulu for walks up in the Talai woods beyond the farm, but we always had our hearts in our mouths going through all the smallholdings, and we kept him firmly on the leash. For some time he had refrained from attacking anything, and Mr Nightingale had not brought up the subject again.

Virginia, whom I had met several times in the town, asked me to go and have lunch with her and George van Tonder. She told us both that Conn was now very ill, and had recently had more than one haemorrhage. She was taking a nurse back with her, but felt it was only a matter of time, and would we both go down if he did suddenly die. About a week after this George sent a message to the Jeffcotts asking me to phone him back immediately. He said that Conn had died that morning, and would I take him down in the office car – he did not drive – to the funeral which was on the following day. The office car had a gear change on the wheel which I had never even seen before, but we consulted the book of instructions and soon got the hang of it. We arrived in Hermanus for lunch, to find Virginia and a very nice nurse waiting for us. Poor Virginia, we were her only real friends at the funeral as, with Conn being so ill for a long time, they had not been able to get to know many people in Hermanus, and all their near relations were in England. We left again about five-thirty, as we both felt we should get home, George, as he worked very hard, and me, because Betty had not been too well with continuous goes of tonsillitis. Virginia was coming up to Cape Town to break the news to Sarah, and said they would both come out for the weekend.

Soon after this, Mr Nightingale broached the subject of Zulu again, saying that Mr Jeffcott kept on about it, so he felt something must be done. We could not possibly move again, even if we could have got a house, which were then unobtainable, so I took the plunge, though hating myself – 'selling my best friend down the river' – so to speak. I advertised him free to a good home, and received thirty-eight answers. They took some weeding out, but eventually I got into contact with some people called Trautman. They lived at Hout Bay, a small fishing village, way beyond Camps Bay. Mr Trautman apparently owned a fishing fleet, and was at sea quite a lot. Mrs Trautman was a nice woman, but I doubted if she would be able to cope with

Zulu on her own. She assured me that her daughter, who worked in Cape Town, came home every weekend and loved to walk and was also very good with, and fond of, dogs. I had taken Zulu with me for this interview and they seemed so keen on him, and it was certainly an ideal set-up for him. Their house was situated quite high, overlooking the bay, with a large garden; and, apart from the village, there were no smallholdings in the vicinity. So in the end, I agreed to let them have him on the condition they would let me know immediately if he did not settle. We took him over at a weekend when the daughter was there. They were both so nice, and realised how we were all feeling. Mrs Trautman gave us a picnic lunch and masses of roses, but when the time came to tie Zulu up on the stoep and desert him, we were all overcome; particularly when he howled as we drove away. Still, a message came in a few days through the Jeffcotts, that he had settled, and that all was well. Soon after this, I got a cable saying that Mummy and Charles had arrived safely, so I felt a bit happier.

Betty did not seem at all well, and the doctor warned her, if she got another attack of tonsillitis, she should have to have them out. We both dreaded the thought and complications, quite apart from it being an unpleasant operation when you are no longer a child.

In the meantime, I felt we must have a dog, and had some absurd idea that if I went to the pound where the strays were kept for a week before being put down, we might find something that would be fun for the children without us getting too involved emotionally. I could not have made a greater mistake as far as that was concerned. The man in charge said he only had one possible, and she was a half-breed Alsatian. I told him a breed like that was impossible after what had happened over Zulu, but he insisted that she was quite exceptional, and by far the easiest and best behaved dog he had ever had there; also, she was in perfect condition and he was at a loss to know why she had not been claimed, and tomorrow was the seventh day. He let her out of the kennel, and she came straight up to us, licked our hands and leapt into the back of the car. Of course we were all lost, so I agreed to have her on a week's trial. We called her Lassie as she had a thick great coat like a collie, and was much more

The boys with Lassie

the size of one too. She settled down as if she had never lived anywhere else. She was so easy too, ignoring all other dogs and only growling if I clipped my fingers and indicated I did not like whoever came to the house. In the town I could take her with me without a lead, and she never left my heels. I was amazed that anyone could lose such a dog, and not try to claim it back.

After three weeks, much to my dismay the Trautmans wrote a letter saying that, after all, Zulu was proving more than they could cope with. Apparently he had taken to going down to the village on his own – not enough exercise I guessed – and pinching meat from the cottages. This had resulted in endless complaints from the Africans who lived there. I had asked them to let me know if there was any trouble over him, as I felt it would be better to put him down, rather than keep passing him on. But they begged me to consider a proposition that had been put up by a young South African naval man they knew. He was stationed at Simonstown, but often spent his weekends with the Trautmans and had got very attached to Zulu. He suggested taking him to Simonstown to become the 'mascot' there. 'Nuisance', their famous Great Dane had recently died, and they wanted a replacement. He had been buried with full naval honours, and during his lifetime had become quite a legend. He was originally owned by a bachelor in Cape Town, who had trained him to give himself his dinner out of the fridge. The alarm clock was set at 5.00 p.m. and when it went off, Nuisance would open the fridge door, take out the bowl with his food in his mouth, put it on the floor, shut the fridge door with his paw, and proceed to eat. He was eventually adopted by the Navy when his owner had to leave, and from that time on would have nothing to do with anyone unless he was a sailor. He had a bed in the hostel, and two season tickets on the train to Cape Town (he took up two seats). I had often seen him walking round the streets in Cape Town: a magnificent fawn dog, but totally uninterested if you made any advances. Apparently, at closing-time, when the sailors emerged from the pubs rather the worse for wear, he would get them by one of their trouser legs and gently lead them to the train for Simonstown. I could hardly see Zulu being able to live up to this paragon, but I did feel that he would be well fed, and be in the company of men who would not be nervous of him and therefore, if he was treated like Nuisance, get as good a life as possible. So I agreed to let him go on trial. I longed to go and see him but felt this would not be fair on him. I heard after a few weeks that he had settled down very well, was a great favourite with all the men, was given lots of meat and exercise, and was sleeping in Nuisance's bed: but unlike him, he did not venture into Cape Town by train, and preferred going out in any lorry or truck belonging to the base. So I really felt I need not worry about him any longer, though I missed him a lot and felt I had betrayed him.

This thought also occurred to me about Lassie. I knew the time would eventually come when we would have to leave her. It would be very difficult to attempt to take a dog back on a troop-ship, which we were most likely to travel in, and even if it could be arranged there was the six months quarantine at the other end. Still, I felt this bridge would have to be crossed when I came to it. All the same, I feel it is a terrible thing to get an animal to have complete trust in you, and then to go off and desert it. This had only happened to me once before in Singapore. After our beloved Oscar had died of jaundice in 1939, we had no replacement and had gone home on leave. On returning to

Singapore in 1940, we had gone to the Dogs' Home there and got a semi-Airedale called George. He was quite a nice dog, but for some reason we never got really attached to him. So when I finally had to leave, I did not feel too badly about him as he was quite happy with the Chinese servants. Of course, what happened to him after the Japs took over, I never heard, and only hope he did not end up on their plates. I suppose, because of George coming as a stray, that I got the idea that Lassie would be the same. But she was certainly not.

Virginia often came for the weekend with Sarah, when she had her out from school. I was very fond of Sarah, but she was getting to be a difficult age, as she no longer wanted to play for long with the children and preferred to sit and listen in to their mother's and my conversation. Betty was very good with her, and would take her off for walks with the others. Cecilia turned up one Sunday, when they were there, with a lovely little pony called Snow White which, of course, all the children fell for and wanted to ride, but she was pulling a tiny governess cart and everyone had rides in that instead. Another time, Virginia suggested we went miles away one weekend to a lovely and almost deserted place called Komatze Beach. We cooked our lunch there among the sand dunes, and then walked a long way to find sea deep enough to swim in, as the tide went out miles. When we got back to the car, ready for the return journey, Virginia managed to break the ignition key – which also opened the boot – and so there we were, stranded. We left Betty in charge, and she and I set out to look for help. Finally, by some cottages, we found two men who had been fishing, sitting in their car eating sandwiches. We explained our plight and they were very helpful, coming along with us and at once getting to work, lying full length under the dashboard. Finally, they started the engine by joining some wires together, but with strict instructions to Virginia not to stall the engine on the way home as we would not get it started if she did. So we were all thankful when we finally arrived back at the cottage.

Virginia and I took Sarah back to school in our car the next day, leaving the others at Wynberg. I went to a dressmaker, where I had a dress and bikini to fetch, and after lunch we decided to go to a film. I had also got some laundry in the back of the car, and, although I locked it, I left one of the windows open a scrap as otherwise it became like an oven. On coming out of the cinema, I noticed at once that the back seat had nothing on it; everything had been stolen. We went to the police to explain, and they told us it was a very easy trick, as the thieves merely had to put a bent wire through the open window and pull up the handle. All the same, they held out some hope of getting my things back as they were all marked, and the new dress and bikini had my initials embroidered on them. Also, they were on to a 'gang' who had used the same method several times before. Even so, I was somewhat surprised when a few days later I got word to go to the Head Police Station in Cape Town, and found they had got *everything* back. Then, apart from having to suffer some pretty ribald remarks over the bikini, which was typical of the South African police, I was horrified when they announced quite casually that they intended to keep the lot as evidence, and the case was to go up to the Supreme Court probably in a month or two. The 'gang' who were responsible were a pretty fearsome-sounding trio, two men and a woman, who they hoped to get gaoled for some years. In the meantime, I said, 'Would it not be possible for me to take the two garments, as I want to wear them, and leave all the laundry with you?' After a lot of discussion over this, I was eventually taken to the Attorney General's Office, and he was most sympathetic and agreed immediately. But I would have to go back in a few days time to identify my belongings in front of the accused. They turned out to be the most awful looking cut-throats imaginable, and they all looked as if they would not mind having a go at me the moment they were free. I hoped that would not be before I was well away from the country.

Valerie had her third birthday in bed with the measles. Mark had been the first to get them but, as usual, was not nearly as bad as the other two. Betty had been going to school on her own, but when Valerie and Rory succumbed together, Hoddie – as we now called her – insisted that she stayed and helped me over the worst. They looked so pathetic, simply covered in spots, and Rory with quite a high temperature for a few days; but they were soon over it, and quite cheerful the moment they could get outside again. Valerie had been born on 12 December, four days after Pearl Harbour, and the first air raid on Singapore. It seemed as if we had been here longer than three years, but we both hoped that by the following Christmas we would be back home with our husbands, though I think Betty had more or less given up hope for Peter. I still felt it was possible that he might be somewhere other than an organised POW camp. A letter came from Uncle Arthur, saying he thought it likely that the European war would be over by the spring, so if then I felt it would be a good move to come home, he suggested I put our names down for a troop-ship sailing around that time. There was one, we discovered, in May, so we booked on that and found the Hills, and various other friends were doing the same. It seemed incredible to think we might be on our way in a few months. Mummy and Charles were looking for a house of their own, but not finding it easy with no car, but we could go to Roper's mother, also in Sussex, and she said we could then have her lodge, as the people there would be out by the spring. Betty intended to go to her mother who lived in Brighton, so we would all be heading in the same direction.

Both Doff Barton and Ruth Van Tonder had produced girls, so I went to see them. Poor Ruth, though thankful it was over as she had felt ill all the nine months, was *so* disappointed it was not a boy, as George was set on having a son; but the Bartons, as it was their first, were both quite content. It was nice to be back in Camps Bay, and I met all our friends who were still there. The twins were both away at boarding school, and Amathe Northy was doing a secretarial course. We had thought of joining up and renting a villa in Hermanus over the Christmas holidays, but the one Virginia had earmarked for us fell through, so we decided to scrap the idea. I was quite pleased, as the measles had pulled the children down. Rory, in particular, had lost a lot of weight and had also had a go of tonsillitis. Our doctor from Wynberg said his tonsils were very enlarged, and agreed it would be better if we had a quiet time and spent Christmas at Bervliet. The Hills gave a huge Christmas party, which I did take the children to. It was a great success, with Cecilia giving rides on Snow White, and almost more mothers than children.

On Christmas Eve Mrs Jeffcott asked me over to meet her daughter-in-law and two grand-daughters, one of which Betty had taken to the ballet. They were all so nice and friendly, and the next day took the boys and me to the service at Constancia Church, while Betty stayed behind and cooked our Christmas dinner. Even Valerie, normally not a very good 'doer', tucked in, and the boys seemed completely recovered from their illnesses. The following day the Ouvrys gave a barbecue for fifty, which the children enjoyed, though I felt was all a bit overdone. Too many people and too much food and drink. Still, I was elated at receiving a letter from Noel and Roper's mother, both giving the same news that some men, who had survived a shipwreck and eventually got back to England, apparently knew that both Roper and Dukie were in Number Four Camp in Thailand with the rest of the regiment, and that Roper was running the canteen. This really seemed to be authentic first-hand news, though one wondered how it had got out, as the men had not been in Thailand. The year ended with a New Year's Eve party at the Van Tonders where I spent the night, but luckily it was not too wild and I quite enjoyed myself.

1944

I WAS HOME by 9.30 a.m. and we spent the day preparing for Mark's birthday party on the third. Seventeen children came, including Trudy with Jane and John. Mark wanted to dress up as Father Christmas, and was a great success appearing over the roof with a sack of presents which he threw down to the children below. To achieve this, I had to see him up a ladder from the back of the house, and was terrified he would trip up on his long 'robe', my dressing gown. But all was well, and he impressed the other children with his daring, which was good for his ego.

The children quite got over all their ills during the holidays, which were quite long, being the South African summer, and we went down to St James's with the Caldicotts' boys and other children to bathe and picnic. We took Betty over to Camps Bay to spend a weekend with the Bartons, and the boys were thrilled with Doff's baby, who was adorable. We saw the Van Tonders on our way home and, while I stayed and talked to Ruth, Olga, now thirteen, took the boys swimming.

Hoddie asked me if I would take some of the older children once a week down to the pool at St James's to teach them to swim. The pool was a natural one in the rocks, and the train stopped just beside it. All the same, it was quite an undertaking on my own, as there were at least sixteen children wanting to go. It took about twenty minutes to get there, and they had to undress behind the rocks. They were so undisciplined that I had to put on a pretty fierce image to keep any control, but they seemed to enjoy it and I managed to survive.

The doctor told Betty that it was essential that she had her tonsils out, so I suggested to Hoddie I would, if she liked, give up my other work and help at the school during the period that Betty was away. Before she went, I spent a few days at the school getting to know her routine and the babies she was in charge of, and I started teaching cricket to anyone who wanted to join in as there were no organised games. Poor Betty had a sort of premonition that things wold go wrong for her in hospital and, as it turned out, she was right. She had bad haemorrhages after the operation, and even I was not allowed to see her for the first two days. When I did, I was so shocked at her appearance, as not only had they broken a front tooth, but had cut her tongue which was so swollen she could not speak. She was in a very weak state and worried about Valerie, but I was truthfully able to assure her that she could not have been easier, and was quite happy at the school, and with me and the boys. The fourteen days in hospital seemed much longer to both of us, but at last she was strong enough to come home, though the doctor insisted that she would not go back to the school that term. So we reversed our roles, though, because she could not drive, I took the car to the school every day and did the household shopping during the lunch hour or on the way home, and Betty would go for strolls with Lassie and cook our high-tea ready for when we got home. Hoddie was very kind and flattering about my coping with the children, and wanted to pay me whatever she gave Betty, but she would not accept my refusal, so we gave it, instead, to the Red Cross. I enjoyed playing with the little ones, which included Valerie of course, though I did not like the job of peeling oranges for them for their mid-morning break. But I had the assistance of a nice coloured girl, who took on this chore quite willingly and much more efficiently. The Matron, who usually took the half-hour rest after lunch, suddenly disappeared, so I found myself in charge instead, also answering the telephone and interviewing prospective parents, as Hoddie refused to be disturbed between two and three in the afternoon.

I had another postcard from Roper during this time, posted in June; only seven months in reaching me instead of a year, but although he said he was 'all right', it was sent from a sanatorium instead of the usual camp. There was an exclamation mark after this, so I concluded he had obviously been ill and hoped the exclamation meant he was better, or just wanted me to think so? Just before Betty was ill, the little Ouvry girl, Juliette, had got glandular fever. This can be fatal, and both her parents were very worried about her, but she seemed much better and had had no temperature for weeks. Then, just after Betty went into hospital, Susan Ouvry fell off her pony and broke her leg in two places. Arthur was in a great state as Juliette was not at school because of her illness. I said I would take her to our school with me, and she could help with the little ones. Then their maid left and Katie produced a temporary one, but according to Arthur she was hopeless and burnt everything. He was not the type to suffer in silence, and was always appearing after I got back from the school – often on horseback – complaining and issuing orders to me. As I was looking after his child, and had three others to feed when I got home, I could gladly have murdered him at times. He sounded so rude, though I realised it was partly because he was worried about Susan and just could not cope on his own. Susan came out of hospital just before Betty, and was able to have Juliette with her, though she could only just hobble around with her leg in plaster and on crutches. After Betty was at home she helped them quite a bit, and often had Juliette with her.

By the time the Easter holidays arrived and we thought things were looking up, Rory developed chicken-pox and the other two followed in quick succession. Three infectious diseases in nine months was a bit too much, we felt. But the last straw was when I developed it too. I had never had it as child, so had a rather worse go than the others, while Mark, as usual, got away with about two spots. Once I had recovered, we all went off to the sea every day and we were soon back to normal, though both Betty and Valerie not a hundred per cent.

The Andreas had braved it and gone off on a ship that left in March, but most of my friends were all hoping to leave on the troop-ship in May, which we were booked on too. It was hard to make up one's mind that it was the right thing to do, but gathered if we did not take this chance, we might have to wait for a long time. Letters from home all seemed to urge us to come; even if the European war was not completely over, they seemed to think it was imminent. So I went to see 'Auntie Gerrard', in charge of the shipping side of the Service Office, and she assured me that our names were on the list, and also that it would be a new ship with excellent facilities for children, though probably very crowded.

Virginia came and spent the weekend and confided that Bunch Keays, an old flame about her own age, who she had nearly married before she met Conn, had appeared on the scene from the Sudan where he was in the Defence Corps, and wanted her to marry him. I had met him once at Camps Bay when he was on leave and thought he was rather like Noel, and had liked him very much. Virginia felt it was too soon after Conn's death, and told him they would have to wait at least another six months, but I felt Conn would not have minded, especially as he had known and liked him, and knew Bunch was still in love with her. She promised to have Lassie if we did go in May but, if she married and went to the Sudan, would have to leave her behind. She had some great friends in Hermanus called Codrington, who were very dog-minded and they had said they would have her, and she knew they would look after her well. I hated the idea of her being passed on from one to another, but she was obviously a dog who could adjust herself, and I felt it was the best I could do for her. I wished I could take her with me, but gathered this was impossible on the same ship, and she might have a terrible time any other way. While Betty and Valerie stayed at the school, I took the boys and Lassie to stay with Virginia in Hermanus so she would get used to the house and Virginia, although she already knew and liked her. We had a good time and got back feeling much better. We told the Jeffcotts and Hoddie that we might have to depart rather suddenly, as we understood that we would only be given a week's notice. Virginia and Ruth, and George, all wanted one or two of my better bits of furniture, and George said he would dispose of the rest after we had gone. This was a tremendous help, and meant we could stay on at the farm almost to the end.

Hoddie said that Betty could take all the children to sleep at the school for the last night or so, and I could go to the Van Tonders if I liked, but I felt I might be better off in a hotel in the town so I could see to any last minute necessities. Betty and I seemed to be endlessly having to go in to the Services Office to fill up forms; typical red tape, but I thought we had no right to grumble as we were getting our passages free. On 24 April we were told it might be only another week, but the whole operation was shrouded in secrecy. I was given a paper pattern for life-jackets, as the ones issued were far too large for a small child, and even capable of breaking their necks if they had to leap any distance into the sea. So I had three, and painted on them their names and home address in large black letters. All rather a grim thought, but there would still be U-boats about.

The word came to get ready, so Betty and I packed what we could, and I got someone to professionally pack the glass and china, as I was taking it all with me as a nucleus to start up with, when we got home. Betty then went to the school, and I spent two nights with the Ouvrys because of Lassie. Virginia was to pick her up from them the day we left, and would spend the last night with me at Arthur's Seat Hotel. I had a farewell party with the Jeppes, Marischel and Cecilia, and Marjorie Hill who was also coming on the same ship with the Olivers. Then, of course, we were told the ship was delayed for a day or two, so I went out to the school and took all the children and Betty out to Camps Bay, mostly to say goodbye to the Bartons as she was still tied with the baby. The Northys had already departed back to England, so, apart from the Olivers who were waiting at the hotel, there were none of our old friends left. It felt very strange, and we hated saying goodbye to Doff and Sven, who had been so good to us all, and helped so much in the early stages. They, of course, would be staying, but Doff felt the twins must go back to see their parents in England and hoped to get them on the next boat after the armistice.

When we arrived back at the school, we got a message to say we were definitely going the next day. Hoddie was out and I hung about as long as I dared to say goodbye to her, but she never turned up before I had to leave, as Virginia would be waiting for me at the hotel. I had rung the Ouvrys to find out how Lassie was, as she had been there far longer than anticipated, but they said she had attached herself to Juliette and they both seemed very happy. I told them that Virginia would be out the next day to collect her, and would be bringing a white rabbit for Juliette – as she had expressed a wish for one, I thought it was the least I could do. Virginia was waiting for me with the rabbit secreted in her bedroom. We had a quiet dinner together, and both hated having to say goodbye. She had been by far my best friend since I had been in South Africa, but she hoped to get home as soon as Bunch had finished with the Sudan; probably in a year's time. She had made up her mind to marry him in the near future, but assured me that the Codringtons were keen to have Lassie and it would be a permanent home for her. She left early, so I did not see her again, and then I was rung to say it would be one more day before we left. The Van Tonders took me to some friends – the Abrahams – for dinner that night, definitely the last farewell party, I hoped. It was all too emotional and upsetting. They insisted that I must come back with Roper and, of course, I naturally hoped that we would be able to.

The next morning it was at last definite that we were to go, and Marischel picked me up at 9.00 a.m. and then we met Betty and the children at the station. He then saw us on board, and so it all went smoothly and we found we had a good cabin. Marischel at last departed, and I felt drained from all the farewells. We found that the cabin had a sixth occupant, a poor old girl who seemed completely bewildered and did not even seem to realise where she was going. We had to take her up on deck with us for a boat drill, and she hadn't a clue what it was all about. Betty and I rather wondered about her, and in particular when, on the first night out, we woke to find her standing over Valerie with a terrible look on her face, repeating 'I *hate* little girls, but I *love* little boys,' We felt she might murder Valerie. So the next day I went to the purser to say I did not think her a suitable person to be mixed with small children, as obviously she was a bit deranged, to put it mildly. The purser seemed to know nothing about her, and asked me to try and find out. All she had on her one suitcase was 'Miss Thompson, passenger to England', which seemed a bit strange. I asked her if she knew where she was going – by this time she had accepted the fact that we were on our way to England – and she said, 'I don't remember dear, but the address is somewhere in my bag.' She handed me her vast handbag and told me to look, but I could find nothing. In the end we all had to move to an identical cabin, but on the other side of the ship, and poor Miss Thompson was given five other women to share with her. I felt bad about deserting her, and she seemed so upset and bewildered when we departed, but we felt greatly relieved to be given a very sane and nice young nurse, who was doing a job and whom we only saw at night.

The Olivers, Marjorie Hill and a friend of hers, Margaret Evans, and myself shared a table at meals with two unattached men, a Colonel Miles and a Captain Best-Dalison who was in command of the naval draft on board. He knew an aunt of Roper's, and said he was an old Etonian 'dressed up as a naval officer – RNVR'. He was good company, so we had quite amusing meals which made up for the food, which was pretty terrible. The children all ate together at another earlier sitting, and Betty had lots of other 'nannies' to keep her company, and particularly liked the Hills' and Evans' nannies, though they were both older and more die-hard than herself.

On 8 May we got the news to say the armistice had been signed. We had been expecting it, but all the same could not believe it was really true. Great rejoicing all round, and a service was held on deck in brilliant sunshine and they fired a twenty-one gun salute, which terrified all the small children, but delighted the boys. They were having a terrific time, and it was almost impossible to keep track of them. They were almost always on the lower deck with the Air Force personnel, who played games with them and fed them endlessly on sweets. This I felt was all right as they were kind and a nice lot of young men, but I did draw the line when I found that Rory had been allowed out onto a platform that was slung out over the sides of the ship to enable them to paint it. Rory protested that he was helping.

The ship was meant to be 'dry', but quite a lot of surreptitious drinking went on in the cabins. Everyone, including myself, had come on board with a bottle or two, and it was all very harmless, relieved the monotony and made one feel rather daring as it was not allowed. The snag was that the cabins were so hot, and one just dripped.

In the daytime, when I was not helping Betty or with the children, we played deck tennis after tea when it was cooler. We stopped at Freetown to get in stores and pick up a few passengers. One of these was a Peter Stevens, who was Second Consul in the Belgian Congo. He found me sitting in my deck-chair – we all had our own, with our names printed on them – and announced he knew Roper's Aunt Olive, and Bertie Young. He was another Marischel type and very friendly, and introduced another man called Rushworth. He was in the Ministry of Transport and said he had met me once in Singapore, and seemed to know and have a great admiration for Roper.

We were told we could have our portholes open, which made all the difference to our nights, and was a great relief. Also, that we were going to Gibraltar to pick up a convoy, as apparently a lot of U-boats had failed to surrender. This would add another four days or so on to the voyage. John Best-Dalison had a radio in this cabin and what seemed to be an endless supply of drink, so we often visited him in the evening and listened one evening to a wonderful speech of Churchill's. My two bottles of brandy were long finished, but Peter Stevens said he had some whisky which we drunk together in a secluded part of the deck. It was cooler there, but more risky, and I had told him that really I did not like whisky so it was wasted on me. All the same, I found it gave me a great 'lift', and so, as I told him afterwards, '11 May was the day I got my first taste of it, and had never looked back since,' We sat up late one night with John and one or two others, including a sweet old man called Sir Duncan Mackenzie who regaled us on his views of marriage, which we did not all agree with.

They were in need of help in the nursery, so I went there every morning to amuse the little ones, including Valerie. She rather missed the boys' company as they were fully occupied elsewhere, and really in very good hands, but of course they all got together at meals and at bedtime.

I would often go and talk with Miss Thompson, who told me some hair-raising stories about the five women who she now shared a cabin with, and asked me to go and see for myself. I knew one of them slightly, a rather saturnine-looking woman who said she was engaged to someone called Gordon of the Gordons. I had not heard of him, but she insisted he was with the regiment in Singapore, but had escaped and was now back in England. I did go down to the cabin one night about seven, and was slightly horrified to find all five women lying on their bunks drinking, while Miss Thompson was dressed for bed and trying to go to sleep. They were taunting her to come out and have a drink too, and seemed to have little sympathy for her. She then leapt out of bed, pulling her suitcase from underneath, opening it and started to rummage inside.

I tried to help her and asked what she was looking for, to which she replied, sotto voce, that she was looking for her dagger so she could kill the lot of them. Of course they overheard, and there were shrieks of laughter which only made her madder. I calmed her down and said not to worry, we would soon be home, and got her back to bed, and departed, knowing she was in the wrong place, but there was little I could do about it.

We arrived at Gibraltar on the 16th to pick up our convoy. Our speed would be reduced to fourteen knots, instead of the twenty-one that we had done up to then, so we were going to be later in arriving than first anticipated. Still, there it was, and I could only hope all would go well for the rest of the time. It was quite a thrilling sight to see so many ships gathered together in one spot, and there were five destroyers to escort us, which was a comforting thought. We hung about all the following day, and only Service personnel were allowed to go ashore. John and another man got back only in the nick of time, as the gangway had been pulled up and they had to climb a rope ladder, much to the amusement of us females who were watching the proceedings. John, immaculate as ever in a white silk shirt, had bought us a gift of some fresh strawberries, but had been forced to tuck these into his shirt in order to have two hands for the ladder. Consequently, of course, they leaked, and made terrible red stains on his shirt; all the same, we enjoyed them at dinner.

We sailed about seven that evening. My heart sank when Mark said he felt ill, and I found he had a temperature. All the same he was able to look out of the porthole and see the exciting sight of a whole lot of other ships steaming along beside us. It was now light quite late, and still warm, so we were able to sit on deck after dinner and admire our new view.

Mark's temperature was up to 102 the next day, so I asked the sister to look at him, and she confirmed, what we thought, that he had tonsillitis, I asked if the doctor would give him M&B, as I knew of old this was the only thing that would get him well quickly. But the sister was quite shocked at the very thought, and said the doctor would never agree to it. So I told her to forget about it, and she retired protesting. I knew exactly what I was going to do, but it always takes a bit of nerve to overrule the medical. Margaret Evans had told me she had M&B in her trunk and would get it for me from the hold, which was quite an undertaking, finding the trunk among hundreds of others and then delving for the bottle of pills. Still, she did, and Mark was as right as rain within a few days. When I did come face to face with the doctor I felt quite pleased at taking things into my own hands, as he looked like an old drunk.

There were a lot of scary and wild rumours flying around about the U-boats, and our destroyers dropped quite a few depth charges. We were then told that we would arrive on the following Tuesday, the twenty-second. We began to feel very excited when the coast of Ireland was sighted on the Monday. It looked now as if our luck would hold and seemed incredible that at last, after four long years away, we were about to arrive home. Some of the convoy left us to go up to Glasgow, while we were to dock at Liverpool. There was quite a farewell party that night, and the Olivers handed me back the life-jacket that I had lent them for their baby. We wondered what the world would have said if we had been torpedoed and drowned, but a small baby with 'Roper-Caldbeck' written on its jacket had survived. Mary had been so distressed at not having one small enough, that I had taken the risk of giving her Mark's, as he was meant to be large enough to fill the ones issued. It seemed so odd that we were all about to be scattered to different parts of England, and it might be some time before we met again.

We sailed up the Mersey, and were tied up alongside a wharf by 10.30 a.m. The rest of the day was spent in sending telegrams, joining vast queues for the immigration people, and finally buying our railway tickets for the journey south the next day. We were told to be ready to leave the ship by 7.30 a.m., but it was more like nine, and then there was the utter chaos when once ashore, trying to find one's luggage. I managed to get hold of the forwarding agents, Cox & Kings, who undertook to handle our big stuff, and the rest the army took down to the railway station, including ourselves sitting on top of the suitcases in an open truck. Here we waited about for hours for someone to allot the seats, but eventually we were able to buy sandwiches and sank down exhausted – all except the boys, who thought the whole proceedings very thrilling – in our carriage. We finally got going at 3.00 p.m. I had phoned Roper's mother, and she had advised us not to attempt to stay overnight in London, but to try and catch the last train down to Haywards Heath (this was three miles from where she lived at Scaynes Hill), where she would have a car to meet us.

We finally got to London at 9.30 p.m. and, by that time, even the boys were worn out. At first I thought there was no getting across to Victoria, as there were no taxis. I left Betty in charge of everything, and came across an empty army truck with two cheerful looking chaps in charge. I told them our story, and that we were desperate to get across to Victoria. I could have hugged them both, as without any to-do they had the children, luggage, and Betty and I all in the truck, Betty and Valerie in the front with the driver, and the other chap and the boys and myself in the open back. Luckily it was a fine night, and it seemed amazing to find ourselves driving through such familiar surroundings, though so much of it devastated by bombs. Somehow, with the help of our army friends, we just managed to catch the train. It was full of Canadian soldiers, and the ones in our carriage, on hearing where we had come from, plied us with sandwiches and joked with the boys. Betty and I were almost past speech, and both Valerie and Rory soon passed out in a dead sleep.

Betty had decided to go on to Brighton and her parents, so when we eventually arrived at Haywards Heath – almost impossible to distinguish in the dim light – we had to leave her and Valerie, and dash to get our luggage out on the platform. Rory weaved around like a drunk, and I could hardly get him to stay upright. But an old porter emerged, and finally the driver, who mother had sent to meet us. We arrived at the house more dead than alive, but I came to life when I found my mother there too to welcome us. We all fell into bed and slept until about ten the next morning. It was sheer heaven to look out of the window to a lovely English spring morning and garden, and to realise our travels were over. Now it was going to be a time of waiting for the Japanese war to finish and for Roper's return. The general opinion seemed very hopeful that it would all be over by the autumn at the latest. My mother departed back to Selsey after lunch, as she did not like to leave Charles any longer. They were negotiating to buy a house there, as they had found it quite impossible without a car to look elsewhere. I said I would bring the boys down to them as soon as possible, but without a car it was quite a business getting to places. Roper's sister, Julia, came over the next day, and took us to see a camp where she worked. It was for POWs from Germany, who were brought there when they first returned. She was in the WVS and was helping to get these men settled. Many of them were Poles, so couldn't go back to their own country.

The boys soon found their way around and loved playing in the wood behind the house, which was over twenty acres and belonged to Mother. They also made friends with Bishop, her gardener, and his terrier called Buller. Old Bishop was rather a forbidding old man, but he was surprisingly good with the boys, and I was much more frightened of him than they were. Mother's brother, Uncle Bertie, came down every night from the London office, only going to his own home in Dorset at weekends. The boys were very intrigued with him, especially when he visited them in bed. He did the most realistic copy of a dog barking, and often finished by presenting them with a half-a-crown each.

Mother's car had been laid up during the war, but she felt the time had come to put it on the road again, although she did not want to drive herself. This was going to be a great help, and of course I would be able to take her about, and get myself to the station and shops in Haywards Heath. Aunt Rose had written to suggest I went up to London to have lunch with her, and having agreed on a date, both the boys got temperatures the day before I was to go. Mother insisted that she could cope, with Mrs King, who was a marvellous person and had been there for years with her husband as a couple. She was a very good cook, and that alone endeared her to the boys and they seemed perfectly happy at being left. I was thrilled to be in London again, and was amazed at how normal things looked, and at the amount of goods in the shop windows. I walked from Victoria to Harrods, and from there up to Hyde Park Corner. I realised then how many holes there were and terrible looking burnt-out buildings, but the sun shone and everyone seemed very cheerful. I took a bus to Oxford Street, and then walked down South Molton Street to Claridges, where I was to lunch with Aunt Rose. I felt quite overcome with her kindness, the marvellous food, and the general grandeur of the hotel with no apparent signs of war. After lunch, she took me up to their suite – more super luxury – and she agreed that *this* was the place where Roper and I *must* stay for the first few days when he eventually got home. I refused to even think what it might cost. When I at last arrived back, I found the boys, far from fretting at my absence, entertaining various people to a marionette show.

We eventually managed to pay a visit to Selsey, and by this time my mother and Charles had moved into the house they had bought. This was right on the sea, with lovely sands. It was a long coast and so one could walk for miles, but the country was very flat and uninteresting and there was a lot of building going on. Not for me, I thought, but for them it was different and had the advantage of an easy walk to the village, and not being too isolated. Joan appeared for lunch, and it was marvellous to see her again, and looking so well and happy. She had fallen in love with a RNVR officer called John Howe, and they hoped to get married as soon as they were both demobbed. The boys fell for Joan, as children always did, and she could not get over how they had grown up, as the last time she had seen them was in London on our way out to Singapore in 1941.

I had quite a day the following Sunday, as Aunt Rose and Uncle Arthur came down from London for lunch; also Roper's brother, Terry, who had just arrived back from Italy, where he had been doing some secret mission away for his regiment, the Argylls. His wife, Marian, was in America, where she had bought a house in Maryland, ready for Terry's return from the wars. Mother had got a temperature and had been ordered to bed, so Mrs King and I were having to cope on our own. As the visit was treated rather like royalty, I was horrified when Terry arrived on his own from the station, having apparently, but unknown to him, pinched the car that had been sent by Mother to meet them all. When the others finally arrived they were slightly ruffled by the delay, and Terry was made to feel he had not been very tactful, but everything soon calmed down and the rest of the visit was very successful. I personally found them both very easy to get on with, and thanked God that the boys appeared in quite a good light, and Mrs King, as usual, gave us a marvellous lunch despite the rationing. It was hot enough to sit in the garden and they all visited Mother in turn, and when they departed the boys were given ten shillings each, which seemed a princely gift in those days.

We had a day in Brighton with Joan, but Betty and Valerie failed to join us as planned, as the latter had a temperature. We had a hectic time visiting the pier, boating lake and fun fair, and finally a 'Punch and Judy' Show on the beach. This intrigued the boys, as they had never seen one before. We arranged to go and visit Joan at her flat in Southsea the following weekend so we could meet John. He turned out to be marvellous with the boys – he was a schoolmaster as a civilian – and provided them with paints and brushes, getting down on the floor with them with huge pieces of paper. Then we four went out to the boating lake, leaving him to cook the lunch. This turned out to be a feast with all the things to gladden a small boy's heart. Soon after this they both came over to Scaynes Hill for the weekend, and everyone there was enchanted with John.

We discussed what we were all going to do in the future, and I told them of my plan to rent a house in Norfolk ready for when Roper came home. We decided that it would be a good idea if Joan and John, once they were demobbed and married, which they hoped would be quite soon, were to come and share the house with us, anyway until Roper got back. John could tutor the boys, which seemed a good idea. He had had some trouble with his kidneys and been advised to take it easy for a time when he was first demobbed, so this seemed to suit us all. Betty said she would come and stay and look after the boys, so I could go up to Norfolk and try and find a house. Roper's great friends, Lance and Florinda Lloyd, lived in a Mill House at Taverham, and had told me to go and stay any time I wanted to. So I wrote to them, and also to the MacDougalls, whom I had met in South Africa and who had said they might have a free house on their estate at Cawston. Cecily MacDougall wrote back to say that they had got an empty house, which had been built for their farm manager who was now living elsewhere. I had told her about our arrangements with John and she suggested that, if he would take on her son, Quinton, as well, they could use the schoolroom at the hall. This sounded quite a good idea, except for the fact that we remembered Quinton as a rather spoilt boy and, to the boys' amusement, was called by his mother *Tinty Poo.*

In the meantime we moved down to the Lodge, as the people Mother had rented it to for the war had left. It was very cosy, and we all had a tiny bedroom each. The boys were thrilled with it, although I had cold feet at having to cook again after such a long interval, and sampling Mrs King's delicious meals; I soon got over that, and it was fun to be on our own again. Mother had her sister, Mabel, and her daughter, Margaret, staying at the house. Margaret, whom I got to know and like very much, often came up in the evenings to see me along with Uncle Bertie. He could come up and have long chats, telling me some fascinating stories about his childhood at Garroch. He was the youngest boy, and Uncle Arthur the eldest. In between were four sisters, Edith, Margaret, Mabel and finally, Alice, Roper's mother and the youngest, so she and Bertie were very fond of each other. As well as these, there were three step-brothers, as their own mother had died soon after Mother was born, and their father, Jasper Young, had married a widow – a Mrs Hannay who had three sons. Sandy Hannay eventually married his step-sister, Edith, which rather complicated things when trying to sort out the family. Bertie had married Olive Annesley and had two children. Peter and Pam, but Peter had died quite early on in the war. He was in the 4th Hussars and had not been killed fighting, although he was with his regiment in North Africa, but had died of rheumatic fever. This had been a terrible blow to them all.

We met Joan and John for a day in London, and John took the boys off to Hamleys so Joan and I could shop. I went to see the gunsmiths, Grant & Lang, and I learnt from them that Rossons of Norwich, where Roper and I had both left our guns, had been blown up. So I asked them to make a new one for Roper, ready for his return. They then showed me a second-hand lady's twelve bore, with two inch cartridges, which they persuaded me was a very good buy, so in the end I fell for it. They made quite a fuss over my visit as all Roper's family patronised the place, and were remembered since they were small boys. Terry had already been in, and they were hoping that the other three brothers would soon follow.

Betty and Valerie arrived at Rock Lodge to take over while I went up to Norfolk. On returning I planned to spend two nights in London, and from there to go straight down to Selsey for a few days. The boys were blissfully happy with Betty, and Valerie with the boys, so I had no qualms at leaving them.

The train to Norwich was full of American troops, and took six hours. It was marvellous to be met by Florinda, looking more like a cheeky pixie than ever, and as full of fun. They were very old friends of Roper's whom I had got to know and love during our first leave home. In fact, we had spent the first month in a farmhouse near to the Mill at Taverham, where they lived. The most memorable thing there was having a hip-bath in front of our bedroom fire. The Mill was at the bottom of the drive up to the Hall, which was a boys' prep school. Richard, their son, was there, and, later, our boys also went to it. Florinda said Lance only came home at weekends as he was stationed at Cromer with the Home Guard. She and I talked into the night, and planned to hire a car and go over to Cawston the next day. I rang Cecily MacDougall who invited us to lunch, but as it happened, Lance turned up unexpectedly so I went on my own. Herbert MacDougall was in a nursing home – it turned out later he was an alcoholic – but Cecily had a very good looking Colonel there who seemed very much at home. After lunch he took me down to see the house, which turned out to be nicer than I had anticipated. It stood on its own, near the entrance to the Hall, with a large expanse of lawn and looking over fields. It was fairly new, and had the right accommodation for us, and was well laid out. Afterwards, Cecily took me round the hall, and showed me the enormous and most attractive school playroom, and outside a fascinating boathouse on the lake, built like a Swiss chalet. I told her I would definitely like to take the house, and could we move in September – it was then the beginning of June. So that was more or less settled. I gathered that *Tinty Poo* was spending the day with friends and Ronald, the older boy, at boarding school.

I got back to the Mill at tea-time, and found Lance there with various troops he had brought over with him to fish in the gravel pits. These were a new addition to me – they were dug out during the war on the common land Lance owned in front of the Mill. There were trout in the Mill pool and the stream, and soon after Lance had departed an RAMC Major, who was stationed up at the Hall, turned up to fish there, and Florinda suggested I went and joined him while she got the supper. It was a lovely evening which I enjoyed, but it was a long time since I had done any fly fishing, so spent most of the time catching the bank or getting my cast into knots.

The next day, we went into Norwich and I was horrified to see the amount of bomb damage. I went to the Museum to see Conn's 'heads' which were magnificent specimens, and a great many of them. We also saw an exhibition of Cotman's paintings, and bought Rory a second-hand bicycle, so went back to the Mill feeling we had achieved quite a lot. The Major, who was at the Mill fishing again, offered to take Florinda and me over to Cawston the next afternoon, as she wanted to see the house, and I needed to take some measurements, etc. The following morning I borrowed her bike and went over to Lenwade, where Roper had been brought up, a matter of six miles or so. I went through the village of Attlebridge, and could see the farmhouse just off the road where we had spent most of our first leave. The Rowlands, who kept the garage in Lenwade, greeted me like a long lost friend, wanting to hear all the Roper-Caldbeck family news as they had known them for years. Mrs Rowland came from Devon and still spoke with a broad accent. She was fat and jolly, and quite excited over some labrador puppies which she thought would just do for 'Mr Reggie' (Roper). She insisted on taking me over several fields to the farm to see them, and she got so out of breath, and talked so much, I was afraid she might have a heart attack as her face was scarlet. When we eventually arrived, the puppies turned out not only to be yellow – when she had assured me they were black – but a cross with collie. Even so, the farmer wanted fifteen pounds for them, but I managed to get out of it, by saying that I knew Roper particularly wanted a black one.

On the way back, this time through the village, which was longer but better walking, we were hailed by an old man who was sitting outside his cottage in the sunshine. This was old Arty, who had lived in the Home Farm when the family had lived at Lenwade Lodge. I had met them on our leave, and he seemed thrilled when he realised who I was. Of course I was considered a 'foreigner', but he had such regard for all the Roper-Caldbeck family, and in particular Roper's mother, who he considered 'an angel', he told me. He took us inside to see Mrs Arty, who I gathered had gone 'a bit queer', but seemed lucid enough that day and quite realised who I was. We talked about old times, and Wilfred Dann, his nephew, who had helped out as a young man as under-keeper and married Anna, who was a housemaid at the Lodge. I told them that we had kept in touch through the war, and that I would be paying them a visit before I left. They were both so keen that I would give a message to Mrs Caldbeck and Miss Julia, that they were 'living for the day when they could both visit them'. Our visit to Cawston went off quite well, and Florinda approved of my decision to take the house, though was a bit amused at the set-up at the Hall where we were given tea. She and Lance had just met the MacDougalls and apparently there was a bit of gossip over Cecily and her Colonel, though we could hardly blame her with Herbert being as he was, and apart from that, I felt it was no business of mine how she conducted her private life.

I returned to London the following day, and stayed two nights at the Normandie Hotel in Knightsbridge. The Olivers – or Onions, as they were still were – had a flat opposite the Brompton Oratory, and they took me to the theatre and out to dinner when, after a few drinks Mary and I (she had asked me to gang up with her) got Dick to promise to change his name to Oliver. Mary felt their two sons would be badly ragged at school and, apart from that, hated the name herself. The next night I went with Terry to Quaglino's, and sitting at the next door table was Miles Reilly with a friend, Willy Twisdon. He was the sweetest man, a regular soldier, and still a bachelor at fifty all because of me, or so he maintained, but then he was full of the nicest kind of Irish blarney. He lived in Ireland and promised to look out for a pony for the boys. I had lunch with him the next day, and I also met Mary Brooke who said that she had had postcards from Charles to say he was interned in Changi Gaol. Then I had tea with Nancy and Alec Fairlie who had recently arrived from

Australia, where they had spent the war as Alec had not been accepted for the navy – he had been a regular Royal Naval officer before coming out to Singapore to a firm of merchants; a great friend of Roper's, and our Best Man. He had been very ill when they were in Australia on leave when the war started, so had stayed on there for the duration. They were now proposing to run a chicken farm in Hampshire. It was rather wonderful how gradually one was meeting up with friends, considering all the different parts of the world where we had spent the war. I went down to Selsey to Mummy and Charles for a few days, and one hectic one with Mummy in London, meeting up with the Hills and Andreas for lunch, and finally to the Olivers to collect some luggage I had left there. I bought myself a brown suit and hat to meet Roper in, and then Mummy and I parted, she to Chichester, and I back to Scaynes Hill where I found everyone well and happy, and no ghastly dramas in my absence.

Betty still had had no news at all of Peter, and was obviously very upset that everyone else we knew had at least had one or two postcards from their husbands, or definite news that they were dead. But the uncertainty of knowing nothing was desperately depressing, and although she was bright enough in the daytime with the children, she got very upset in the evening when we were on our own. I still felt there might be a slender chance that he had escaped onto an island in the Pacific, while being taken up to one of the POW camps in Japan. There were rumours that one ship, at least, with our POWs on board, had been sunk by our own people, and that there were survivors who had got ashore. She and Valerie had to leave to go back to Brighton, as her mother had rung her to say her father was very ill. We missed them a lot, but I managed to get a nice girl from the village, who came in the mornings mainly to help with the washing. This gave me time to give the boys some schooling, as I did not wanted them to forget everything they had learnt at the Little People's School. All the same, I did not find it a very easy task, and they resented being kept inside on lovely sunny mornings when they wanted to be out in the wood. Mother was out at meetings most days, and Julia very busy at the camp, but I saw quite a lot of Margaret.

On 10 August, the news came that the Americans had ended

the war with Japan by dropping an atomic bomb on Hiroshima with horrific effects, but personally it was difficult to feel anything but intense relief that it was all over and, with luck, the POWs would soon be on their way home. It would obviously take some time, and we waited impatiently for news. At last we were told that the ones who were in Thailand were to be flown out to Rangoon, and that both Roper's name and Harry's were on the list of survivors. Then an airmail letter came from Roper himself. He was in Rangoon hospital, but made great light of his condition and said it was merely routine, although he had had dysentery for the last two years which had been partly cured by some drugs that had reached the camp six months previously. His weight now was nearly twelve stone, having been down to half that, but he seemed to think his present weight was partly due to the drugs and unhealthy fat which, although they had saved his life, had not been sufficient to complete the cure. The worst cases were to be flown home, but he, Harry and Dukie and the rest of the regiment were coming by troopship as it was considered that the voyage would do them good. This would take three weeks at least, but they hoped to arrive early October.

I was on top of the world, and rang Joan to tell her, and we decided to go ahead with our plans and move up to Norfolk early September. She and John were now free, so it was arranged with Cecily MacDougall that we would come almost at once. She was providing the basic furniture, and I had brought quite a lot of stuff with me from South Africa, and acquired a bit more locally. Joan and John arrived in the furniture van as they had quite a lot of their own stuff, so had loaded it up at Southsea, and we set forth the next day. The boys thought this was a great adventure, and sat at the back with John, sitting in armchairs, while Joan and I and a labrador puppy, Brutus, I had just acquired, sat in front with the driver. We said a fond farewell to Mother and everyone at Rock Lodge, but knew we would all be meeting again soon when Roper and Harry arrived.

It seemed quite a long journey, but we arrived eventually and found Cecily had had the beds made, and got some basic food in. We settled down very happily, and John wasted no time in getting the schoolroom equipped, and was soon setting forth every day after breakfast with the boys up to the Hall, where they were joined by Quinton. Cecily was charming and most helpful. Herbert was home again, but was always trying to waylay John in the 11.00 a.m. break, or when they finished at 12.30 p.m. and get him to visit the cellar with him on the pretence of showing him his vintage wine, but it usually ended up in them sampling one or two, and often being caught in the act by Cecily who obviously was very disapproving. The Gamekeeper and his wife were a sweet couple called Pocock, and lived down a lane near the house. Joan and I went there for eggs, and were regaled also by a certain amount of gossip. We gathered that Herbert hit the bottle hard, despite his time being cured, and that Ronald, the older boy, was rather a difficult character and not very popular with the locals and staff.

John was asked to shoot pheasants one Saturday, and we all turned up to help beat – except Cecily and Quinton, who seemed to suffer from a permanent cold. The country was flat, but made attractive by large areas of wood and parkland.

Two sisters ran a very efficient riding school not far down the road to Aylsham, and the boys often went along with John, or me, in the bus on Saturday mornings for riding lessons. Although they had ridden a little in South Africa, I thought it was good idea for them both to get a bit of proper grounding, especially as Miles Reilly had written to say that he had bought a dark bay pony mare, which he was sending over as soon as he had got over the shipping formalities, which were a bit complicated.

The Olivers were going back to Rhodesia, and wrote and asked me to go up to London to see them before they left. As I wanted to book the suite in Claridges and to see to one or two other things before Roper arrived, I decided to go up for a couple of days, and Joan and John were quite happy about my leaving the boys in their charge. I had asked Herbert Rowland, at the garage in Lenwade, to look out for a second-hand car for us as we really had to have one, although the local bus service was quite good and passed right by our front door. Herbert came out to fetch me to go into Norwich for the train as he ran a taxi service, and said he had heard of a Citroen which he thought might be quite a good buy, and he hoped to be able to vet it in a day or so.

I went to the theatre both nights with Mary and Dick, and then said a sad farewell to them over a last supper. The next morning I happened to notice a shop in Knightbridge which looked rather like an Eastern Bazaar, with oriental rugs hanging outside. We badly needed some floor covering, so I went in to enquire. The shop was run by a charming ex-RAF man who said all the stock was owned by a friend, who was returning to America and wanted to sell the lot cheaply, to get rid of them quickly. I felt there must be a catch somewhere, especially when he said if there were none there suitable, he would take me to his friend's flat around the corner where there were hundreds more. I presumed he had been stationed in the Middle East, but was not prepared for the amazing collection to be seen at the flat. A key had been thrown out of the window when my friend from the shop whistled, and we climbed long stone steps leading to the third floor. When we got there, it was just like the Arabian Nights, and I wished I had longer, but by this time, I had one eye on the clock as I was catching the only past midday train to Norwich. I picked up a small rug which I liked, and asked the price, which was a modest seventeen pounds. The man in charge seemed completely off-hand about the whole transaction – if I was buying several, obviously it would have been a different matter. Anyway, he said a cheque was all right, but then neither of us had a pen, so I wrote it in pencil and, with the rug under my arm, and the original chap with my suitcase, we rushed down and managed to get a taxi almost at once. I caught the train by the skin of my teeth, and by the time I calmed down and began to reflect, I realised what I had done. What was to stop them altering the seventeen pounds to seventeen thousand pounds. I rang my bank the next day to stop the cheque if it was more than the right amount, but I need not have worried. Moreover, I have been told that it is a particularly good example of a Persian rug, and it is still going strong decorating our dining-room hearth.

Finally, I got a cable from Roper saying he was arriving in two days' time. I managed to get a reply off to the docks at Southampton to say, 'Come to Claridges.' He rang that morning to say he would be in London by five the next day. I took the early morning train, and went straight to the hotel. I told the manager that Roper would be arriving that afternoon, and he said that he would be the first returning Jap POW they had seen at the hotel. There seemed to be quite a lot of excitement at the thought.

Nothing to what I was feeling; but it was nice to think that an establishment that was trained to show no emotion was capable of a little excitement. I was sitting in the grandeur of the drawing-room of the suite after lunching with Mary Brooke, who had flown in case Roper turned up earlier than expected, and has asked a waiter to come up so I could order the dinner – anything to pass the time – when there was a knock on the door and there, in his old kilt and black hobnailed shoes, stood Roper. Everything froze, then the waiter dropped the menu and with the chaps who had shown him up, they hurriedly departed, leaving us alone, and there we were together again; the impossible had come true.